OINS AND COINAGE.

THE

TED STATES MINT,

PHILADELPHIA,

'ORY, BIOGRAPHY, STATISTICS, WORK,
ACHINERY, PRODUCTS, OFFICIALS.

eces of Gold, Silver, Nickel, Copper, Brass

AND THEIR VALUE.

TOKENS, MEDALS; COLONIAL, NATIONAL, STATE, INDIVIDUAL:
ESPECIALLY RELATING TO THE PAST AND PRESENT
OF THE UNITED STATES,

DESCRIBED AND MARKET PRICE QUOTED.

ILLUSTRATED MOST PROFUSELY.

PHILADELPHIA, PA.:
A. M. SMITH, PUBLISHER.

FOURTH EDITION, REVISED AND ENLARGED.

ILLUSTRATIONS.

PAGE

Annapolis Shilling, 1783.....................90
Annapolis Sixpence, 1783..................91
Annapolis Threepence, 1783.............91
Automatic Weighing Machine...........27
Baltimore Town Piece........................91
Bar Cent, 1785..................................96
Bland Dollar.......................................71
Brasher's Doubloon, 1787.................99
Carolina Elephant..............................93
Casting Ingots.................................. 16
Cent, 1808..84
Cent, 1816..85
Cent, 1856-59.....................................86
Cent, Bar, 1785..................................96
Cent, Chain, 1793...............................81
Cent, George Clinton, 1787...............48
Colonial and Continental Notes.....113-116
Cent, Colonies Francoises, 1722.........94
Cent, Colonies Francoises, 1767.........95
Cent, Immunis Columbia.............98-105
Cent, Kentucky................................110
Cent, Talbut Alum Lee.....................100
Cent, Washington...97-105-106-107-108-109
Coining, Middle Ages........................11
Coining, Presses...................12-13-25
Coining, Punch A. D. 337.................10
Coins Connecticut.............................101
Coins, New England 88
Coins, Summer Island........................88
Colonial Coins......................88-112
Copper, Excelsior, 1787..............97
Coppers, Inimica Tyrannis, 1785...104
Coppers, New Jersey.........................102
Coppers, Vermont 100
Coppers, 2 cent piece, 1864.............80
Counting Board...................................29
Cutting Press....................................20-21
Dies...26
Dimes..76-78
Dismes Half Dismes, 1792....................5
Dollars, Gold....................................66
Dollars, Silver 67-70
Double Eagles....................................57
Draw Bench 19
Eagles, 1745-1870.............................58
Excelsior Coppers, 1787...................97
First Steam Press, U. S. Mint.............12
Five Dollar Gold Coin 59-62
Franklin Cent....................................111
Fugio Cent...111
George Clinton Cent, 1787 98
Georgivs Triumpho Copper, 1783......109
Gold, Brasher's Doubloon, 1787......99
Gold Coins, U. S 57-66
Granby Copper...................................89
Half Cent......................................86-87
Half Dimes Silver, 1796-1835...........78
Half Dimes Silver, 1838....................79
Half Dismes and Dismes, 1792.............5
Half Dollars.................................72-74
Half Eagles...................................59-62
Higby Coppers...................................17
Ingots..16
Ingot Casting 16
Immunis Columbia, 1787 98
Immunis Columbia, 1786 105
Inimica Tyrannis, 1785 104
Kentucky Cent.................................110
Kentucky Token...............................110
Libertas Americana...........................45

PAGE

Liberty Cap Cent, 1793.....................82
Liberty Cap ½ Cent...........................87
Liberty Cent, 1799............................84
Liverpool Half Penny.......................106
Lord Baltimore Money......................90
Louisianna Coins.........................94-95
Machine, Automatic Weighing..........27
  "   Coining 11-13
  "   Milling 23
  "   Rolling 17-18
Mark Newby Cent 92
Massachussetts Coins, 1788 103
Maryland Coins 90
Medals, National..............38-40-42-44
Middle Age Coining 11-13
Milling Machine 23
Mint U. S. Philadelphia 14
Mind Your Business.........................111
Mott Token, 1789 99
National Medals 38-40-42-44
New England Sixpence 88
New Jersey Coins.............................102
New York Cents..................................97
Nickel Coins..................................79-80
Nova Caesarea Copper.....................102
  "   Constellatio, 1785.................104
Non Dependens Status, 1773...............96
Oak Tree Money, 1652........................89
One Dollar, Gold................................66
One Dollar, Silver........................67-70
Penny, Rosa Americana................94-95
  "   Half Virginia..........................95
Perforated Strip.................................22
Perfected Coining Press....................13
Pine Tree Money................................89
Pitt Token, 1766................................93
Press Cutting................................20-21
Quarter Dollar...................................74
Quarter Eagle....................................23
Rosa Americana, 1723-1738 93-94
Rolling Machine.................................17
  "   Gold.......................................71
Shilling, Annapolis 90
  "   New England 88
Silver Coin First American 88
  "   Coins, U. S............................66-79
Steam Press U. S. Mint......................12
Strip, Perforated...............................22
Summer Island Coin...........................8
Ten Dollar Gold Coin 58
Trade Dollar, 1880.............................70
Three Dollar Gold Coin.....................65
Three Cent Pieces, 1870....................79
Twenty Cent Piece, 1875....................76
Two and Half Dollar Coin.............59-62
Two Cent Pieces, U S.........................80
Threepence, New England...................89
Threepence, Annapolis.......................91
Town Piece, Baltimore.......................91
Token, Pitt, 1766................................93
Token, Rosa Americana.......................93
  "   "   "   1738......................94
  "   Kentucky..............................110
  "   Mott......................................99
  "   Talbut Allum Lee 100
Virginia Half Penny...........................95
Vermont Copper Piece........................
Vermont Victoria, 1788......................
Washington Cent ....
Wreath Cent, 1793.............................

3

TABLE OF CONTENTS.

	PAGE
Adjusting Coin	22
Alloy of Cents	86
Alloy of Nickels	79
Amount U. S. Coinage	5 to 9
Ancient Coins	34
Annapolis Tokens	91
Arizona Gold	9
" Silver	9
Assay	28 to 31
Assorting Machine	33
"Auctori Plebis" Token	109
Australian Coins	34
Baby Head Cent	85
Baltimore Town Piece	91
Bar Cent	96
Biographies	48 to 56
Bland Dollar	71
Blondeau Piece	11
Bosbyshell, Col. O. C.	55-56
Brasher's Doubloon	99
Brass Money	88
Brown Moses	8
British Settlement Kentucky Coin	110
Cabinet of Coins	32
" " Medals	34-48
California Gold	9
" Silver	9
"Carolina Elephant"	92
Cent "Bar"	96
" "Baby Head"	85
" "Chain"	81
" Copper and Nickel	80
" "Fugis" or "Franklin"	111
" "Jefferson Head"	85
" "Kentucky"	110
" "Liberty Cap"	82
" "Massachusetts"	103
" "Plicæ"	83
" "Silly Head"	85
" "Tory" Head	101
" Washington	105
" " N. Y.	97
" " Double Head	106
" " Large Head	106
" " Large Eagle	106
" " Naked Bust	107
" " President	106
" " Small Head	105
" Wreath	82
" Worth of Sets	86
Chain Cent	81
"Cob" Money	84
Coining	9-48
" Ancient	10
" By Steam	11-13
" Room	24-27
" Press, Latest	12
" Punch	10
" in Vermont	100
" in New Jersey	102
" Massachusetts	103
" Department	55
Coinage of first Eagles	7
Coins, Copper	80-88
" Odd, U S	
" Colonial	8 ...8-112
" Colonies Francoise	94-95
Colorado Gold	9
Colorado Silver	9
Colonial Coins	88-112

	PAGE
Connecticut Coinage	101
Continental Currency Piece	111
Counting Boards	28
Colonial and Continental Paper Money	115-118
Copper	5
Coppers "Confederatio"	103
" "Excelsior, N Y"	97
" "Georgivs Triumpho"	109
" "George Clinton"	98
" "Granby"	89
" "Higley"	89
" "Inimica Tyrannis"	109
Cutting Gold	20
Cutting Press	20
Curiosities, Relics, etc	34
Cuppellation	30
Dakota Gold	9
Deposit of Gold in U S Mint	8
Deposit Melting Room	15
Deposit Weighing Room	15
DeSaussure, Hon H W	41
Dismes	6
Discovery of Gold in North Carolina	8
Dimes, Silver	76-78
Dollars, Edge lettered	66
Dollar of 1804	68
Dollars, Silver	66-71
" Standard	71
" Trade	70
Double Eagles	57
Doubloon Brasher's	99
Draw Benches	19
Du Bois, Wm E	34
Eagles	57-58-59
Eagle vs Goose	7
Eckfeldt, Adam	33
English Silver Tokens	86
Engraving Dies	31
Excelsior Coppers	97
Filing Coins	22
First U S Coinage	5
" Coining Press	12
" U S Mint	5
" Silver Dollars	7
Five Cent Nickel	79
Foreign Coins	34
"Franklin Press" Tokens	109
Fugio or Franklin Cent	111
George Clinton Copper	98
Georgia Gold	9
Gold	8
" Assay	29
" Coins, U S	57-66
" Melting and Refining	15-16
Gobrecht, Christian	
Goose vs. Eagle	7
Granby Coppers	89
Greek Coins	34
Gun Money	36
Half Cents	86-87
Half Dimes	78-79
Half Dismes	5
Half Dollars	71-74
Half Dollar, Washington	107
Half Eagles	59-62
Harman's Vt. Coins	100
Higley Coppers	89
History of Coinage	5-56
History of Philadelphia Mint	5-6-14-56

PAGE

Idaho Gold...............................9
Idaho Silver..............................9
"Immunis Columbia"..............104-105
"In God We Trust".....................70
Ingots 17
"Inimica Tyrannis" Copper...........104
"Jefferson Head" Cent................83
Jefferson, Thomas.......................6
Kentucky Cent 110
Kentucky Tokens 110
Lake Superior Silver....................9
"Large Head Washington" Cent......106
Lettered Edge Coin 84
Libertas Americana Medal..........43-45
Liberty Cap Cent......................82
Liberty Cent 84
Lord Baltimore Money..................90
Louisiana Coins 95
Lyon, Matthew Hon......................7
Mark Newby's Money...................92
Maryland Silver Tokens............90-91
Massachusetts Coins..................103
Maundy Money.........................36
Medals 37
Medals Mount Vernon 39
Medals 1812-1815......................45
Medals Mexican War...................46
Melting and Refining 15-16
"Mind your Business"................111
Mints in New Jersey..................102
Mint U. S. Philadelphia 5-6-14-56
Milling Machines 24
Milling Coin 24
Middle Age Coining 10
Mill and Screw Coining 11
Mode of Coining........................9
Modern Coins 34-35
Montana Gold 9
Montana Silver 9
Morris, Robert..........................7
Mott Tokens...........................99
Myddleton Penny......................110
National Medals 43
New England Elephant 92
    "   "   Shilling.................89
Newby's Money 92
New Jersey Coinage...................102
    "   "   " value...............103
    "   "   Mint....................102
Nevada Gold............................9
Nevada Silver 9
New Mexico Gold 9
New Mexico Silver 9
N. Y. Excelsior Copper................97
    "   " Washington Cent............97
    "   " "Immunis Columbia"........98
Nickel Alloy...........................79
    "   Coins 79-80
North American Token 109
North Carolina Gold....................8
Nova Caesarea 102
Nova Constellatio....................103
"Non Dependens Status".............96
"Nova Eboracs".......................97
Numismatic Publications.............102
Oak Tree Money 89
One Cent Copper......................80
One Dollar, Gold...................65-66
    "   "   Silver 66-71
Oregon Gold............................
Origin of Mill Screw....................1

PAGE

Overstrikes.....................74-76-85
Pattersen, R. M......................12
Perfected Coin Press 13
Pine Tree Money......................89
Pitt Token............................93
Planchets 22
Portraits 32-33
Presidential Medals..................47
Punch Coining 10
Quarter Dollars....................74-76
Quarter Eagles.....................92-65
Rare Coins prices of........113-114-115
Rare Medals..........................87
    "   Silver Dollars.............68-69
    "   Quarter...................74-75
    "   20c Pieces...................76
    "   Dimes........................78
    "   3c Pieces....................79
    "   1c Pieces.................80-84
    "   ½c Pieces....................83
Rittenhouse, David.....................5
Rolling Gold..........................17
Rolling Room.........................18
Rosa Americana Money 93
Scales 15-29-33
Scotch Pennies 36
Seyss' Automatic Weigher............27
Silver 9
    "   Assay.........................29
    "   Coins......................66-79
    "   Pennies...................36-39
Silly Head Cent 85
Small Head Washington Cent.........106
Snowden, Col. A. L...............48-54
Snowden, J R.........................12
Sommer Island Coins.................88
South Carolina Gold 9
Standard Dollar......................71
Superintendent of Mint...............47
Tokens, Mott 99
    "   Washington 105
    "   Talbot, A, and L..........100
    "   English....................109
    "   North American............109
    "   Auctoris Plebis............109
    "   Franklin Press.............109
    "   Continental Currency......111
Testing Metals.......................28
Testing Scales.......................33
Thatcher, Judge......................67
Three Cent Silver....................79
Three Cent Nickel....................79
Trade Dollars........................70
Twenty Cent Pieces..................76
Two Cents Copper....................80
Tory Cents..........................101
Utah Silver 9
United States Mint...................14
Valuable Cents.......................85
Value of Foreign Coins..............120
Value of Jersey Coins...............103
Vermont Coinage....................106
Virginia Gold..........................9
    "   ¼ Pennies.....................9
    "   Shilling......................85
Washington Cents...........105, 106, 107
    "   N. Y........................97
    "   Half Dollar.................107
    "   Bust Piece..................109
    "   Piece with stars over ......
Eagle................................108

HISTORY OF U. S. MINT.

The use of coins as a circulating medium, in substitution of simple barter, has so long been a matter of every-day practice that it is difficult to conceive the existence of a period when their use was unknown; and yet, the invention of coins, as we now understand the term, is a comparatively modern one, not dating farther back than about seven or eight centuries before the Christian era, though different modes of substituting metals and other substances for simple barter had been adopted at a much earlier period.

A coin, let it be found where it may, proves at once several things concerning the people who originally used it, and their state of civilization.

The first coins of the United States Mint were issued in a small three story building in this city, at No. 29 North Seventh Street, between Market and Arch Streets, and near Filbert Street.

On the 31st of July, 1792, at 10 o'clock in the forenoon, the foundation stone was laid for this the first United States Mint, by David Rittenhouse, Esq. The foundation was completed and ready for the superstructure on Satuarday, the 25th of August, 1792, and the frame work was raised in the afternoon of the same day. The building was completed on Friday, the 7th of September, 1792. On Tuesday following, the 11th of September, *six pounds of old copper* were purchased for the Mint at 1s. 3d. per pound, this being the first purchase of copper for coinage.

LIBERTY PARENT OF SCIENCE & INDUS.
1792
UNITED STATES OF AMERICA
DISME
HALF DISME

In the beginning of October, 1792, three presses were put in operation and were first used for striking the half-dismes, of which Washington makes mention in his annual message to Congress on the 6th of November, 1792, as follows:

"There has also been a small beginning in the coinage of
half-dismes; the want of small coins in circulation calling
the first attention to them."

This half-disme has upon its obverse a female bust, emblematic of Liberty, facing to the left. This is popularly supposed
to represent the features of Martha Washington, who is said
to have sat to the artist while he was designing it. The hair
is short and flowing. Immediately beneath the bust is the
date 1792, surrounded by the legend " LIB(*erty*), PAR(*ent*) OF
SCIENCE AND INDUSTRY." Reverse :—Eagle on the wing, beneath the same is inscribed: "HALF DISME." Legend : UNI-
(*ted*) STATES OF AMERICA." This coin is said to have been
struck from the private plate of Washington, which is not un-
likely, considering the great interest he took in the operations
of the infant mint, visiting it frequently, and personally su-
perintending many of its affairs. This half-disme made its first
appearance in October, 1792; but was not generally circulated and has now become one of the rare coins of our national
coinage.*

From 1792 to 1832 there were coined in this modest little
building 132,592 eagles ; 1,925,867 half eagles ; 180,392 quarter eagles ; total gold coinage 2,238,854 pieces. Also 1,440,517
silver dollars ; 59,584,783 half dollars ; 2,506,029 quarter
dollars ; 8,619,600 dimes ; 4,942,647 half dimes ; total 77,-
093,576 silver pieces. Of the copper coins 62,925,602 copper
cents and 6,627,710 half cents were coined, making a total of
69, 553,312 copper pieces, or a grand total of gold, silver and
copper of 148,885,742 coins.

In 1833 the present United States. Mint, located in Chestnut
Street below Broad Street, was completed, and made fire-proof
in 1856. The corner stone was laid by Samuel Moore, Esq.,
Director of the Mint, on the 4th of July, 1829.

The style of the present U. S. Mint is Grecian, of white
marble ; built rather to insure security for its treasure than to
present an imposing appearance.

The Act of April 2, 1792, established the Mint, the money
of account, and authorixed a National coinage. Prior to this
several preliminary steps were taken, and in January, 1782,.
Thomas Jefferson proposed that coins of the United States
shall consist of "ten units to be equal to one penny ; ten pence
one bitt ; ten bitts one dollar ; ten dollars one crown." This
last coin to be of gold. Mr. Robert Morris, the originator of

---

*A "Disme," of double the weight and size, was also coined. It is
now of extreme rarity, excepting in copper, in which metal it is also
scarce

this proposed coinage, appologized·for introducing the name of
"Crown," in a country where that emblem had lost favor, by
stating that his project was to have on the coin the representation of an Indian, with bow in his left hand, and thirteen
arrows, emblematic of the thirteen original States, in the right,
with *his foot on a crown.* Although repeatedly discussed in Congress, no further step was taken till 1784, when the Spanish
dollar was resolved upon as the standard, and upon this basis it
was proposed to strike four coins, namely; "A golden piece, of
the value of ten dollars; a dollar of silver; a tenth of a
dollar, also of silver, and a hundreth of a dollar in copper."
The first golden piece, of the value of ten dollars, called the
Eagle, was coined in June, 1795; its weight 270 grains and 22
carats fine. It bears upon the obverse a female head, emblematic of the Goddess of Liberty, wearing the liberty cap, the
hair flowing loosely. Around the edge of the field are fifteen
six-pointed stars—five on the right and ten on the left of the
same. Legend: "LIBERTY." Exergue: "1795." Reverse:
American Eagle with expanded wings, holding in its beak a
laurel chaplet, and in the talons a palm branch. Legend:
"UNITED STATES OF AMERICA." Of this coinage there is but
one type and three varieties; all of which are very scarce.

The first silver dollar was coined in October, 1794. The
field of the reverse was proposed to be occupied by an eagle.
This question of the emblems and devices of our National coins
was before the House of Representatives, when Matthew Lyon,
a Congressman from the South, warmly opposed the eagle as a
monarchial bird. The king of birds, he thought, could not be
a suitable representation of a country whose institutions were
founded in hostility to kings. In reply Judge Thatcher proposed a goose, which he said was a most humble and republican bird, and would, in other respects, prove advantageous,
inasmuch as the goslings would be convenient to put on the
dimes. The laughter which followed at Mr. Lyon's expense
was more than he could bear. He construed this good-humored
irony into an insult, and sent Judge Thatcher a challenge.
The bearer delivered it to Mr. Thatcher, who read and returned it to him, observing that he should not accept it.
"What! will you be branded as a coward?" "Yes, sir, if he
pleases. I always was a coward, and he knew it, or he never
would have challenged me." The joke was too good to be
resisted even by the angry party.

It occasioned infinite mirth in Congressional circles, and the
former cordial intercourse between the parties was soon restored
in a manner entirely satisfactory. This was a very happy

ending, and it was well said that Mr. Lyon wisely concluded there was no use trying to fight an adversary who fired nothing but jokes.

This silver dollar bears upon the obverse a female head, with loose tresses failing below the neck. Legend: "LIBERTY," directly over the head; seven six-pointed stars around the outer circle of the field, on the right of the effigy, and eight on the left. Exergue: "1794." Reverse: American Eagle, with extended wings, standing upon a rock, encircled by a laurel wreath. Legend: "UNITED STATES OF AMERICA." Upon the edge: ONE * * DOLLAR * * OR * UNIT — * * * HUNDRED ———— CENTS * * ———— * *. Of this dollar there exists but one type, which is exceedingly scarce and commands a considerable premium. The first deposit of precious metal in the United States Mint was a lot of French coins on the 18th day of July, 1794, and was made by the Bank of Maryland, amounting in value to eighty thousand seven hundred and fifteen dollars seventy three and a half cents. Of gold the first deposit was made by Moses Brown, a merchant of Boston, Mass., and consisted of gold ingots, amounting to two thousand two hundred and seventy six dollars and twenty-two cents.

Prior to the discovery of the gold fields and mines of California the supply for the coinage of American gold coins was furnished by parties importing foreign coins, a few stray lots of African gold, and the products of the North and South Carolina, Virginia and Georgia gold fields. The discovery of gold in North Carolina was brought to the notice of this country in 1824, when a traveling merchant passing through a settlement near Ruthford, N. C., noticed quite a large lump of gold ore, used by a farmer in place of a stone to keep the door of his cabin from shutting. The peddler asked the woman how much she wanted for that yellow stone, as he called it, to which she replied that any thing he was willing to make a present to her boy Charlie, who knew where there were plenty of similar yellow stones, would be acceptable. Three silver coins to the value of about two dollars were handed the mother, who was overjoyed with the liberal gift. The merchant soon brought the nugget to a goldsmith who cheerfully paid him a sum equal to about two thousand seven hundred dollars. The name of that liberal and shrewd merchant, thanks to Divine Providence, has been lost to posterity.

Gold is found in various parts of the earth, but is most abundant in Africa, Siberia, U. S. of America, Japan and Australia. In South America gold was first discovered by the

Spaniards in 1492, from which time to 1730 nuggets of gold of various sizes and grades were shipped to Europe, when in that year a nugget equal to sixty pounds troy weight was found near La Paz, a town of Peru. Gold was discovered in Malacca in 1731; in New Andulasia in 1785; in Ceylon in 1800; in Virginia 1829; in North Carolina 1824; South Carolina 1829; in Georgia 1830; in California April 1848, and in Australia in April, 1851. In 1858 gold was discovered in what is now termed New Columbia, British America.

The deposits of gold of domestic production made at the U. S. Mint, the different branches and assay offices from the earliest period to the present day, January 1, 1881, include a value of $702,058,970.35 from California; $48,689,006.09 from Montana; $35,417,517.54 from Colorado; $24,137,417.11 from Idaho; $14,432,322.55 from Nevada; $15,414,509.57 from Oregon; $7,698,082.03 from Georgia; $7,235,112.89 from Dakota; $10,613,351.10 from North Carolina; $2,256,742.06 from Arizona; $1,672,667.70 from Virginia; $1,569,472.14 from New Mexico; $1,401,845,30 from South Carolina.

Silver exists in most parts of the world; the silver mines of South America, prior to the vast discoveries in the U. S. of America, were by far the richest, although in Russia, Spain, Germany and Norway a considerable amount of silver was found mixed with other ores, such as copper, lead, etc. In 1660 a mine was discovered in the district of La Paz, in South America, which was so rich that the silver of it was often cut with a chisel. In 1749 a block of silver was discovered in Spain weighing over 370 pounds. From a mine in Norway a block of silver weighing 560 pounds was recovered.

The deposits of silver of domestic production deposited at the U. S. Mint, the different branches and assay offices from the earliest period to the present day, include a value of $72,107,030.69 from Nevada; $20,183,889.56 from Colorado; $9,036,957.01 from Utah; $3,433,674.78 from Lake Superior in Michigan; $2,221,484.63 from New Mexico; $2,116,717.64 from Arizona; $4,371,384.12 from Montana; $1,677,550.45 from California, and $727,295.50 from Idaho.

MODE OF COINING.

Our knowledge of the mode of coining money in early times is extremely imperfect. As soon as the savage tribes began to improve in civilization, or where driven back by the more enlightened inhabitants, the coins began to show a marked change for the better.

At the earliest period the impressions upon the coins were made by a hammer and punch.

The piece of metal to be coined was first fashioned into a semi-bullet shape; this being placed upon the face of the die, the punch was applied to it and struck with a hammer.

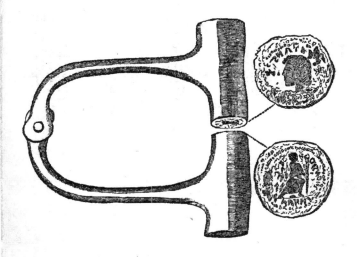

COINING PUNCH.

The one here represented was used by the Emperor Constans, who reigned from A. D. 337 to 350. On the obverse die, the letters STANS are still visible. The reverse has a figure representing Victory, with a Trophy and a palm branch.

In Europe during the Middle Ages coins were made as shown by the cut on the following page, representing a coining establishment in full working order.

In the foreground in the middle are seen the workmen at work preparing the plate to its required thickness by application of vigorous hammering; to the left the man with shears cutting that plate into the required rude shape of a coin, which is then passed to the workman to the right who impresses the same with

COINING ESTABLISHMENT OF THE MIDDLE AGES.

the necessary inscriptions etc., by again applying the hammer to the punch which stamps with force upon the die below.

The mill and screw is of French origin, the invention of An toine Beucher, in 1553. It was continued in use until 1585 when it was laid aside, as it was found much more expensive than the old hammer process. We find no mention of its having been used after this time until 1623, when Briot, a French artist, unable to persuade his own government to adopt it again, passed over to England, where it was immediately put in practice. There, finally after short duration, it was again discontinued, for the same reason as before, and a resort had to the old hammer and punch system. But when the Common·wealth was established, Mr. Pierre Blondeau, a Frenchman, who had carried the most improved modes of stamping coins by the mill and screw to great perfection, took charge of the coining operations at the English Mint. Blondeau, notwithstanding his ingenuity, and his good services to the State, appears to have been badly used by the authorities, although his proces of the mill and screw was continued.

The mill and screw was continued in use in the U. S. Mint until about 1836.

The first steam coining press was invented by Mr. Thonnelier, a Frenchman, in 1833, and was put in practice in the U.S. Mint in 1836, the old screw-press having been used there up to that time.

U S. MINT FIRST STEAM-POWER PRESS.

This press simple in construction, stands about five feet in height, and takes up a space of about four by five feet. On the back of this press is a brass plate, which has the following inscription:

"First steam power press 1836.
Built by Merrick, Agnew and Tyler.
R. M. Patterson, Director United States Mint.
Remodeled and rebuilt, 1858, by D. Gilbert.
J. R. Snowden, Director United States Mint."

This press was used for many years, but finally was replaced by more effective machinery. Its defect was justly attributed to the arch which was fastened to an iron table, and caused too much vibration. A solid arch and other improvements designed and executed by American mechanics obviated soon that vibration and a perfect coinage was the result.

This improved press was used for many years afterwards, but finally had to give place to improved machinery. It was sold in 1874 to Mr. George B. Soley, who exhibited it in Machinery Hall, during the Centennial Exposition, where it was used to strike off the Centennial Medals.

13

PRESENT PERFECTED COINING PRESS.

The present press as represented by the above cut is the perfection of mechanism. Great care has been taken to obviate the unsteady bearing and the continued vibration, and by careful reconstruction after the model and improvements suggested by Col. A. Loudon Snowden, it performs its work by the solid stroke. In this way not alone is there perfection, precision and excellent workmanship obtained, but there is a saving of over seventy-five per cent. in the destruction of dies, which is highly appreciated by the Government

THE UNITED STATES MINT OF TO-DAY.

On the north-west corner of Chestnut and Juniper Streets, below Broad, stands a Grecian style building of white marble somewhat gray from age, with a tall chimney rising from the center in the back ground, and the U. S. flag flying from a staff upon the roof, this is the U. S. Mint of to-day. Ascending a long flight of easy steps, and before entering the building, a placard upon the main entrance door, informs you that " Visitors are admitted from 9 to 12." This door opens into a circular entrance hall, with seats around the wall.

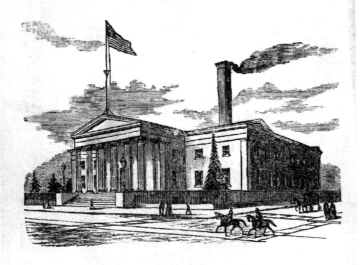

Standing in the rotunda at the entrance, and looking into the building, we have the office of the Warrant and Registering Clerk's of the Mint on our left, and on the right the Cashier's office. A polite and courteous usher meets you at the door, and guides you through those departments of the Mint which are open to visitors, for owing to the immense amount of precious metal which is constantly in course of transition from one form to another, and the care and watchfulness necessary to a correct transaction of business, visitors are not permitted to visit some of the departments.

Passing through the hall leading to the yard the Minor

Coin Redemption room is on the right; a part of this room is used by the Adam Express Company.

On the left is the

THE DEPOSIT WEIGHING ROOM.

In this deposit and weighing room all the precious metals used by the Mint are received and weighed. The nicety and exactness of the scales in this room is quite a study. The scales, large and small, are balanced with wonderful delicacy. The largest scale in this room will weigh from six thousand ounces to the one-hundredth part of an ounce or about 5 grains troy. The next size weighs as much as three thousand ounces, while the smallest weighs as much as three hundred ounces at a draft. These scales are examined and adjusted almost daily. The largest weight used in this room is five hundred ounces and the smallest the one-hundredth part of an ounce; but the smallest weight in use at the Mint is the thirteen-hundredth part of a grain, scarcely visible to the naked eye, except on white ground and in very bright light. This weight is only used in the Assay office. The deposit and weighing room is not accessible to visitors; but through the glass doors all that is of interest can be inspected.

On the right of this room is a vault, of which there are twelve in the building. They are of solid masonary, and several of them are iron-lined, with double iron doors, and the most ingenious and burglar-defying locks.

THE DEPOSIT MELTING ROOM.

When the gold has been weighed in the weighing room it is locked up in iron boxes, provided with two different locks, and is then carried to the melting room. In this room there are several furnaces, and the first process of melting takes place there. Previously to the gold bullion being charged into the pots, the furnaces are lighted by the workmen at an early hour, and the pots gradually annealed, as they are liable to crack by too sudden an application of heat. This is done in the following manner: black lead or plumbago pots, are placed in a series of furnaces, about two feet deep from the grate. On the grate, formed of movable iron bars, supported by cross-bars let into the brick-work, a stand is placed for the pot, this stand is filled with common coke-dust, to prevent adhersion of the pot to the stand. To give depth to the pot in the furnace, and allow of as much fuel as the furnace will hold, a muffle formed of baked clay is placed on the pot in such a manner that the rim of each will fit exactly, and the mouth of the muffle is covered with a flat cover made of black lead.

The object of this contrivance is to give an additional depth of four inches of fuel above the pot, by which a more equal degree of heat is given to the melted gold, an object of great importance, otherwise there might not be a uniform mixture of the alloy and fine gold.

As soon as this deposit is thoroughly melted in a mass, it is cast into a bar; this bar is numbered, and a slip cut from it and sent to the assay department, there, by assaying that slip, the amount of pure metal contained in the entire deposit is ascertained.

ROOMS OF THE MELTER AND REFINER.

In the northwest corner of the building, not far from the Deposit Melting Room are located the rooms of the Melter and Refiner, the refining and standarding of the metals, and

CASTING INGOTS.

the casting them into ingots or small bars from which the coins are to be made, are performed.

INGOTS.

The bars or ingots thus produced are about twelve inches long, half an inch thick, and from one to two and a half inches in width, according to the size of the coin for which they are intended. The weighing of the neccessary quantities of alloy takes place, in the Melter and Refiner's office.

ROLLING MACHINE.

THE ROLLING ROOM.

Passing through the corridor leading to the rolling room, our attention is attracted to an engine of about 160 horse power, which supplies the motive power to the rolling machines. By the aid of these massive machines of which there are several in a row, with their black heavy stanchions and polished steel rollers, the rolling of the gold and silver planchets is performed.

Here the attendant measures two ingots, and shows to the visitors that they are exactly of the same length; hands the same back to the workman in charge of the rolling mill, who

ROLLING MACHINE AS SEEN BY THE PUBLIC.

puts one of them between the rolls, chisel end first, and it is drawn slowly through. He measures it with the other ingot, and we see it has grown about an inch longer and correspondingly thinner. This is the "breaking down." But it is not thin enough, it must be rolled ten times if gold, or eight if silver, to reduce it sufficiently, occasionally annealing it to prevent its breaking. These rollers can be brought very close together and the pressure applied so intense that half a day's rolling heats not only the strips and rollers, but even the huge stanchions, weighing several tons, so hot that you can hardly hold your hand on them. Every rolling mill can be altered to roll any degree of thinness, but usually the ingot passes through several mills, each reducing it slightly. When the rolling is completed the strip is about six feet long or six times as long as the original ingot.

It is impossible to roll perfectly true. Now and then there will be a lump of very hard gold, which will not be quite so much compressed as the rest. If the coin were cut from this place, it would be heavier and more valuable than one cut from a thinner portion of the strip. It is, therefore necessary to " draw " the strips, they first being softened by annealing.

THE DRAW BENCHES.

Our attention is next drawn to a long table, with the odd-looking, endless chain, running from right to left, making a deafening noise, this is the Draw Bench.

DRAW BENCH.

In fact there are two benches, one on each side of the long table. At the right end an iron box is secured to the table. In this are fastened two perpendicular steel cylinders, firmly supported in a bed, to prevent their bending or turning around, and presenting but a small portion of their circumference to the strip. These are exactly at the same distance apart that the thickness of the strip must be. One end of the strip is pinched somewhat thinner than the rest, to allow it to slip easily between the cylinders. When through, this end is put between the jams of a powerful pair of tongs, or pincers, fastened to a little carriage running on the table. When the end is between the pincers, the operator touches a foot pedal which closes the pincers firmly on the strip, and pressing another pedal, forces down a strong hook at the left end of the carriage, which catches in a link of the moving chain. This draws the carriage away from the cylinders, and the strip being connected with it has to follow. It is drawn through the cylinders, which, operating on the thick part of

CUTTING PRESS AS SEEN BY THE PUBLIC.

the strip with greater power than upon the thin, reduces the whole to an equal thickness. When the whole is through, the strain on the tongs instantly ceases, which allows a spring to open them and drop the strip. At the same time another spring raises the hook and disengages the carriage from the chain. A cord fastened to the carriage runs back over the wheel near the head of the table, and then up to a couple of combination weights on the wall beyond, which draw the carriage back to the starting place, ready for another strip.

THE CUTTING PRESSES.

In the rear of the rolling mills and drawing benches are

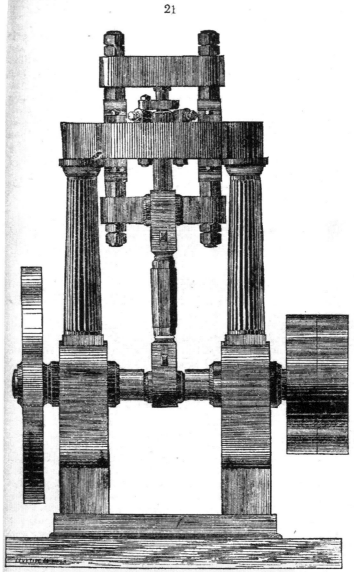

CUTTING PRESS.

This engraving shows the present cutting press, as perfected by Col. A.

There are several of these machines, each one capable of cutting two hundred and twenty-five planchets per minute.

The cutting press consists of a vertical steel punch, which works in a round hole or matrix, cut in a steel plate. The action of the punch is obtained by an eccentric wheel. The operator places one end of the strip under the punch and cuts a couple of round pieces a little larger than the coins they are to make, these round pieces are called " planchets." As the strips are of the uniform thickness, if these two are of the right weight, all cut from that strip will be. They are therefore weighed accurately. If right, or a little too heavy, they are allowed to pass, as the extra weight can be filed off. If too light, the whole strip has to be remelted. As fast as cut

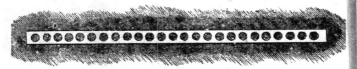

PERFORATED STRIP.

the planchets fall into a box below and the perforated strips are folded into convenient lengths to be remelted.

We next visit the northern end of the Coining Room, where the sorting of these planchets takes place. The planchets are thrown upon a table with two holes in it, and each woman employed here, picks out all the imperfect pieces or chips, which are slipped into one hole, and the perfect ones into the other, where they fall into different boxes.

THE ADJUSTING ROOM.

In this room each lady operator has on the table before her a pair of very sensitive assay scales. Seated close to the table, a leather apron, one end tacked to the table, is fastened under her arms to catch any gold that may fall. In short sleeves, to avoid sweeping away the dust, and armed with a fine flat file, she is at work. She catches a planchet from a pile by her side and puts it into the scales. If too heavy, she files it around the edge, and weighs it again. Still too heavy, files it again, and weighs it. Almost right, just touches it with the file. Right, and she tosses it into the box, and picks up another planchet to undergo the same operation. To adjust a coin so accurately requires great delicacy and skill, as a too free use of the file would quickley make it too

A

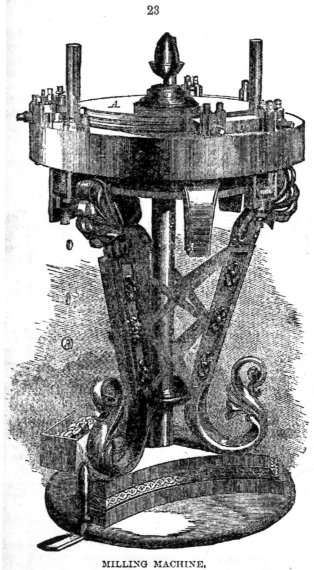

MILLING MACHINE.

light. Yet by long practice, so accustomed do the lady operators become, that they work with apparent indifference, scarcely glancing at planchet or scales, but seemingly guided by their touch.

THE MILLING MACHINES.

At the northern end of the Coining Room are the Milling Machines. These machines are operated by ladies, and are used to turn up the edges of the planchets, before they are ready for the coining press. This upturned edge is only raised a little higher than the device. It is done to prevent the device being worn by rubbing on counters etc., and also that the coins may be piled one on another steadily. This edge is raised by a very beautiful piece of mechanism, and in the following manner:

· Several planchets are placed in one of the brass vertical tubes, of which there are several, for different sized coins. At the bottom of the tube the lowest planchet is struck by a revolving feeder, which drives it horizontally, between the revolving steel wheel on one side, and the fixed segment on the other. · The segment is on the same curve as the wheel, though somewhat nearer to it at the further end. The planchet is caught in a narrow groove cut in the wheel and segment, and the space being somewhat less than the diameter of the planchet the edge is crowded up. The planchet makes four revolutions when it reaches the end of the segment, and being released from the grooves falls into a box below. The edge is perfectly smooth, the fluting or "reeding," as it is termed, being put on in the process of coining.

THE COINING ROOM.

At last the coining room is reached, occupying the greater portion of this floor, on the east side of the building. This undoubtedly is the most interesting department to the visitor of the mint.

A passage-way is separated by a neat iron fence, but the visitor can see every thing from the side of the division. In this room there are several presses, each one capable of coining from 80 to 120 coins per minute; but the large presses are seldom run at a greater speed than 80 per minute. The largest presses are used in making coins of large denomination. The small presses are used for base coins and the smaller denomination of the silver pieces. These machines also are generally attended by lady operators.

The arch of the coining press is a solid piece of cast iron, weighing several tons, and unites with its beauty great strength. The table is also of iron, brightly polished and very heavy. In the interior of the arch is a nearly round plate of brass, called a triangle. It is fastened to a lever above by two steel bands, termed stirrups, one of which can be seen to the right of the arch. The stout arm above it is

COINING PRESS AS SEEN BY THE PUBLIC.

also connected with the triangle by a ball-and-socket joint, and it is this arm which forces down the triangle. The arm is connected with the end of the lever above by a joint somewhat like that of the knee. When the crank lifts the further end of lever it draws in the knee and forces down the arm until it is perfectly straight. By that time the crank has revolved and is lowering the lever, which forces out the knee again, and raises the arm. As the triangle is fastened to the arm it has to follow all its movements. Under the triangle, buried in the lower part of the arch, is a steel cup or technically, a " die stake."

DIES.

Into this is fastened the reverse die. The " die stake " is arranged to rise about the eighth of an inch, but when down it rests firmly on the solid foundation of the arch. Over the die stake is a steel collar in which is a hole just large enough to allow a blank planchet to drop upon the die. In the triangle above, the obverse die is fastened, which moves with the triangle; and when the knee is straightened the die fits into the collar and presses down upon the reverse die. Just in front of the triangle will be seen an upright tube made of brass, and of the size to hold the blank planchets to be coined. The blank planchets are examined by the operator in attendance, and the perfect ones are placed in this tube. As they reach the bottom they are seized singly by a pair of steel feeders, in motion as similar to that of the finger and thumb as is possible in machinery, and carried over the collar and dropping upon the die. The knee is straightened, forcing the obverse die to enter the collar and press both sides of the blank at once. The sides of the collar are fluted, and the intense pressure expands the blank planchet about the sixteenth of an inch, filling the collar and producing on the coin the fluted or reeded edge.

After the blank planchet has been dropped upon the die, the feeders slide back on the little platform extending in front of the machine, in readiness to receive another. The knee is now bent, which raises the die about half an inch above the collar. The die stake is raised at the same time, so as to lift the newly made coin from the collar, and the feeders coming along with another blank, push the coin over into a sloping channel, whence it slides into a box underneath.

A planchet consists of a blank disk cut from a slip of metal prior to being stamped. These planchets although cut from carefully prepared slips of metal rolled out to their exact thickness are often of uneven weight and unfit for the coining press.

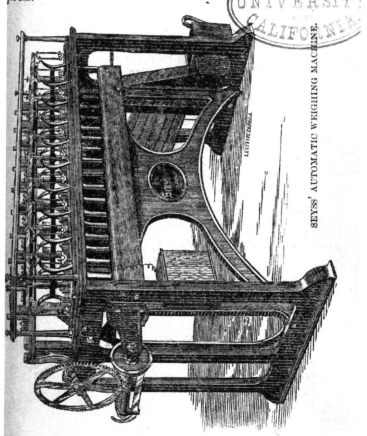

SEYSS' AUTOMATIC WEIGHING MACHINE.

The above illustrated machine which does the work of several young ladies, is of German origin, and is known as the "Seyss Automatic Weighing Machine," named thus after the inventor; it weighs and assorts every planchet or blank disk

This automatic weighing machine was introduced in this Mint by Col. A. Loudon Snowden at the time he was Chief Coiner.

This machine has ten scales, and the gold planchets filled in their respective tubes are forwarded piece by piece to be weighed and assorted.

There are three receptacles, one for the planchet which exceeds its proper weight, and which after having thus been rejected is forwarded to be filed off to the required weight. The second or middle receptacle is destined for the planchet of the exact weight and ready to be acted upon by the coining press. The third and upper receptacle is for the planchet which is too light for coinage and hence rejected, and its destination, the melting pot.

. At the end of this automatic planchet weighing and assorting machine is an electrical apparatus which sounds the alarm bell in case two planchets instead of one should find their way into the box; when the bell rings the attendant immediately remedies this irregularity and the work proceeds. Two of these machines have been in operation for several years, and recently three others have been added. The latter are arranged for making four divisions of planchets, which are termed; "Light," "Light Adjusted," "Heavy Adjusted" and "Heavy." These machines are located to the left of the visittor, on entering the Coining Room.

THE COUNTING BOARDS.

Here are also seen the "Counting Boards," quite curious and useful inventions, which are used only for small silver and minor coins. Twenty-five dollars of the five cent pieces can be counted by this ingenious swift working machine, in less than one minute. These counting boards are a flat surface of wood, with copper partitions the height and size of the coin to be counted, rising from the surface at regular intervals, and running parallel with each other, from top to bottom. These boards are worked by hand, over a box, and as the pieces are counted they slide into a drawer prepared to receive them; after which the counted coins are put in bags, and removed to the office of the Coiner, where they are again weighed. (See illustration page 29.)

THE ASSAY ROOMS

Every bar of gold and silver is properly tested prior to being rolled out into slips. A small piece is taken off each lot by the Assayer and conveyed up stairs to the Assay Rooms, in the southwest corner of the building. On entering these rooms the necessary appliances for the performance of this work great he eye of the visitor. Here we find the most sensitive scales enclosed in glass cases. These glass cases are mostly kept closed when the Assayer is engaged in his work, for a draft of air would influence them and spoil some of the calculations.

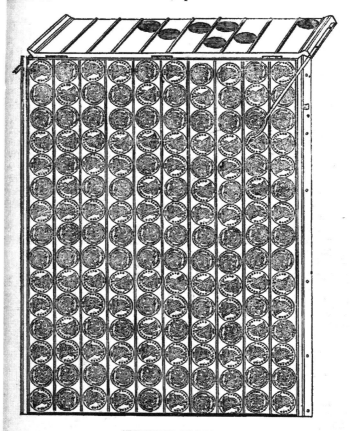

COUNTING BOARD.

Assaying is a mode of ascertaining what proportion of gold or silver there is in alloy of those metals. When an alloy of silver is melted the inferior metals become oxidized, and can be removed as a kind of scale.

The assay furnace is a small upright stove, having within it a wagon-like earthen vessel, called "muffle," closed at all parts except one end, a few slits in the top and side. small crucibles, called "cupels," are placed in the muffle, which shields them from contact with the fuel in the furnace. The cupels are small cups, made of bone ash that will not be acted upon by fused oxides, while their texture is sufficiently porous to let the oxides penetrate.

The process of assay requires that the copper and silver be both entirely removed from the gold; and to effect this, two separate operations are necessary.

The first is for the removal of copper; and this is done by a method called *cupellation* which is conducted in an assay furnace, in a cupel composed of calcined bones. To the other metals lead is added; this metal possesses the properties of oxidizing and vitrifying under the action of heat, of promoting at the same time the oxidation of the copper and other base metals, and of drawing with it into the pores of the cupel the whole of these metals, so as to separate entirely this part of the alloy, and to leave behind the gold and silver only.

The separation of the silver from the gold is effected by a process founded on the property prossessed by nitric acid of dissolving silver, without acting upon gold. But that the gold may not protect the silver from this action, sufficient silver must first be added to make it at least two-thirds of the mass. The process to be described is based upon the rule of *quartation*, in which the proportion of silver is three-fourths.

The object of the silver assay is to determine the exact proportions of fine silver contained in any bullion, plate, or coin.

The assay does not regard the nature or variety of the alloying metals, but simply their proportionate weight to that of the pure silver.

There are two methods of assaying silver, one known as the "dry" or "furnace assay" or "cupellation," the other the "wet" or "humid assay" or the "volumetric process."

The method of "furnace assay" or cupellation, already described for gold, when applied to silver requires such a nice regulation of temperature and so many extreme precautions, and is at best so liable to uncertainty of results, that it is now only used in a subsidiary way, to furnish an approximate result, or a basis for the closer and more delicate manipulation of the humid assay.

The humid assay, with proper care and due attention to the condition of the liquids, may be regarded as a perfect process of analysis for silver, both as respects accuracy and uniformity of results.

The principle of the humid assay is that of determining the proportion of fine silver in an alloy, by ascertaining the exact amount of a known precipitant required to eliminate the fine silver contained in a solution of a given weight of the alloy, so that the result is obtained without a final weighing of the precipitated silver.

The necessary amount of the precipitating agent being found and the weight of the alloy known, the number of parts of fine silver in a thousand is deduced by calculation.

For this purpose a solution of common salt, chloride of sodium, is used.

ENGRAVING ROOMS.

In these rooms the dies are engraved with which all our national coins are stamped. The Chief Engraver's office of the U. S. Mint has for many years been filled with honor by the Messrs. Barber, father and son. Mr. Barber is for the present engaged on the memorial medal of Lincoln-Garfield, a piece of workmanship never excelled by any other artist, and seldom equaled by any engraver in the art of die-sinking.

The preparation of dies for stamping coins and medals is a work requiring considerable skill and care, The steel selected should be of moderately fine grain and uniform texture, and when polished, should show no spots or patches under a magnifying glass. Two short lenghts having been cut from bars of steel and forged into rough dies, are next made as soft as possible by careful annealing, being put in an iron pot with animal charcoal, heated to a cherry red and allowed to cool gradually. After being faced up flatly and smoothly in a lathe they pass into the hands of the engraver, who traces upon them their appropriate images, obverse and reverse, and works these out with steel tools. The new matrices, or maternal dies, when, after repeated impressions on clay, etc., and alteration, they are found correct, are ready for hardening—a process simple enough as regards plain steel, but here very critical, seeing that a delicate engraving has to be kept intact. Each matrix is first protected with a mask. composed of fixed oil thickened with animal charcoal, or of lampblack and linseed oil. They are then placed face downwards in a crucible, and burned in animal charcoal. After

being heated a cherry red they are taken out with a pair
of tongs, plunged in a large body of water, moved about
rapidly till all noise ceases, and left in the water till quite
cool. If the matrix pipes or sings, there is probably a crack
in it. The hardened die is next polished and tempered, the
former by holding it against a running iron disk, coated
with flour-emery and oil, the latter by putting it in water,
which is gradually raised to the boiling-point, then allow-
ing it to cool slowly, or by placing it on a heated bar of
iron till it acquires a rich straw color. To increase its
strength an iron ring may be shrunk upon it, like a mechani-
cal jacket. The matrix, treated as here described, might
now be used to multiply coins or medals, but it is prefer-
red to use it for first producing punches, or steel impressions in relief. With this view a steel block is procured,
softened by annealing, and turned in the lathe, being made
flat at the bottom and obtusely conical at the top. The
block is put in the bed of a die stamping press, and the
matrix brought down on it with force by means of the central screw. Thus a copy is produced in relief on the conical surface. Further strokes may be required to perfect it,
and the punch is therefore first re-annealed, its surface having been hardened by compression, then replaced in the
press; the matrix, detached from the screw, is fitted on to
it, and pressed in contact by decent of a block of steel
attached to the screw. Thus, after repeated blows and fre-
quent annealing, the impression is completed, and after being
retouched by the engraver is hardened and tempered like the
matrix. The matrix is now laid aside, and the punch used
to produce any number of steel dies by an operation sub-
stantially similar to that by which the punch itself was
obtained. These are, of course, fac-similes of the matrix, and
when completed are used for purposes of coinage.

THE COIN CABINET.

The room in the U. S. Mint used for the Coin Cabinet is
on the second floor, is fifty-four feet long by sixteen wide.
The eastern and western sections are of the same proportions,
each with a broad window; the central section is lighted from
the dome, which is supported by four columns.

Entering the Cabinet, the portraits of the different Direc-
tors attract attention, they are those of David Rittenhouse,
a copy of painting by Charles Wilson Peale, the original is
the property of the American Philosophical Society; Henry
William De Saussure, painted by Samuel Dubois; Elias

Boudinot, an excellent copy of a painting by Walds Jewett Robert Patterson, a copy of a fine original by Rembrandt Peale; Samuel Moore, painted from life by Samuel Dubois; Robert Haskell Patterson; Dr. George N. Eckert; James Ross Snowden; James Pollock; Henry Richard Linderman; and the present Superintendent Hon. A. Louden Snowden, painted from life by Mr. Brown.

Among the relics, the first object of interest on entering the Cabinet, to the left, is the framed copy of the law of Congress establishing the U. S. Mint, which was approved by President Washington, on March the Third 1791.

On the opposite wall is a case containing gold plate in strips, comprising gold alloyed with copper, showing the bright hues of deep color, and the gold alloyed with silver the mild, pale tint.

Near the western window and to the right as you enter the room is the Seguier's assorting machine. In this machine the planchets are thrown into the hopper at the rear, and, being arranged by the action of the wheel, slide down balances. By ingenious machinery beneath, they are carried one by one to the nearest platforms to be weighed. If too heavy, the tall needle of the beam leans to the right, and lifts a pallet-wire, which connects with an apparatus under the table, by which the planchet is pushed off and slides into one of the brass pans in front. If the planchet be light, the needle is drawn over to the left, and touches the other pallet, which makes a passage to another brass pan. If the piece be of true weight the needle stands upright between the pallets and the piece finds its way into the third brass pan.

In the eastern section in a large glass case are the "Standard Test Scales" of the United States Mint, which are used to test the weights sent to all the branch-mints and assay offices of the United States, and are so sensitive as to discover the twenty-thousandth part of an ounce. The beam of these scales is hollow, filled with ceder to guard against the ill-effect of dampness; the bearings are perfect edges of knife-blades, which rest on a surface of agate plate. These scales are examined once a year by the annual assay committee.

The collection of coins for this Cabinet was commenced in June, 1838; but long before that time Mr. Adam Eckfeldt, chief coiner, led as well by his own taste as by the expectation that a conservatory would some day be established, took especial pains to preserve master-coins of the different annual issues of the mint, and to retain some of the finest foreign specimens, as they appeared in deposit for recoinage, and consequently have cost the Mint no more than their bullion value. They are, moreover, the choicest of their kind; and perhaps there are few cabinets where so large a portion of the pieces are in so fine preservation, as well the ancient as the modern coins.

The ancient coins are displayed in several cases, mitred in pairs, and placed erect against the walls in the wide doorways and the middle room. The modern coins are variously arranged; part being in a nearly level case surrounding the railing of the open enclosure, which lights the hall of entrance below; and part being in upright cases, disposed along the walls of the middle and west rooms.

The minerals, metallic ores, relics and curiosities are placed in the west room. The ancient coins have been admirably classified by William E. Du Bois, Esq., Assayer of the Mint, and are as follows: Division I, include the Era of the Roman Republic of which there are 202 coins; Division II, from Julius Caeser to Trojan inclusive, 181 coins; Division III, Hadrian to Elagabalus, 149 coins, Division IV, Severus Alexander to Claudius Gothicus, 153 coins; Division V, Aurelian to the End of the Western Empire, 169 coins; Division VI, the Byzantine Empire, 113 coins.

Among the ancient Greek coins we have to record 158 coins of the Greek Republics and 174 coins of the Greek Monarchies.

The modern coins form a very valuable collection, in which the "Colonials" are well represented.

The Cabinet also includes several coins of African coinage, those of the Sierra Leone Company and Liberia.

Of America, Central, North and South, the coins of Bolivia Brazil, Chili, Ecuador, La Plata, Mexico, New Grenada, Peru, Uruguay and Venezuela form the principal collection.

The "Cob" money of Mexico consists both of gold and silver, and is an unsightly coinage, of so rude a character as to scarcely deserve the name of coin. The larger portion of this coinage was issued about 1740 and continued up to 1770. They were struck with a hammer, and are of any form except that of the true circle. Of Australian coinage four coins of gold represent that country; they are quite curiosities on account of their peculiar raised and grained edge, with sunken legends, and raised figures in the field.

Of the Austrian Empire, including the coinage of Hungary, several very exquisite specimens exist in Division VII of the Cabinet.

Belgium proper, forms part of Division VIII, jointly with the coinage of the Netherlands; in this collection is found the famous "*Lion d'argent*" the Silver Lion coin, struck in 1790, bearing upon the reverse the eleven arms of the different Belgian provinces, arranged in a circle around a sun.

Denmark, Holstein, Sweden and Norway form Division XIII, and include some 150 coins of gold, silver and copper. Among the Danish coins is the gold ducat of Christian IV, of 1645, known as the "Justus Judex" coin. It bears upon the obverse the image of King Christian IV, crowned and attired in armor, a scepter in his right, and the imperial globe in his left; upon the reverse the inscription "Justus Judex" in Hebrew characters. In the collection of the Holstein coins is a thaler of Peter, grand-duke of Russia, with the arms of Norway, Russia, Oldenburg, Holstein, etc. Among the Swedish coins of Christian IX, 1610, and Gustavus Adolphus, 1617, we find silver coin containing in Hebrew characters the word Jehovah.

The coins of France form one of the choicest collections in the Cabinet. A handsome Denier or penny of Charlemagne, 767 to 814, A. D., well preserved being over 1000 years old, is among the many coins. A silver medalet of the unfortunate Maria Antoinette, Queen of Louis XVI, having upon the obverse the Queen's bust, an excellent portrait, is also among these coins. The French coins of the different republics, also those of Napoleon the first, are varied and fully represent those momentous times.

. The coins of the German Empire, prior to 1806, the German States and the German Empire of to-day are very numerous. Those especially of the German States from 1806 to 1871, are mostly of Prussia, Saxony, Bavaria, Hanover, Wurtemberg, Baden, etc., etc. Among the older coins of the 17th and 18th century are several very fine gold Medallic Ducats of great beauty and value, prominent among which the Martin Luther Centennial Ducat of 1617; it was coined by John George I, Duke of Saxony. Another Ducat, represents the gold money of the Silver City. This is one of the most remarkable pieces in the collection, as it bears neither date, name, nor other mark, from which its authorship can be deduced, the obverse contains a prayer to "*Christ to save the city*," which, on the reverse is styled the "*Silver City*." Still another gold medallic ducat bears the heads of Martin Luther and Philip Melanchton. This coin is generally very much admired by visitors for its beauty and remarkable portraiture.

The collection of the British coins includes a coin made

head of Minerva, with the famous Greek helmet. Also two small gold coins, about 2,000 years old, they bear no inscription. The first has on one side a representation of the *sun*, with three dots, or pellets, beneath. The second a full length figure of a man. They are somewhat after the Greek style of coins, concave at one side. Also a silver Skeattae of Ethelbert I, King of Kent, 560—616 A. D. Several silver pennies of Burgred, last King of Mercia: Ethelbert I, fourth King of England A. D. 858 to 871, Edred and Edgar, 946 —975 A. D.

Next in interest are two silver pennies of William, *the Conqueror*.

Among the famous English gold coins is a " Noble" of Henry VI, an " Angel " of Henry VII, a " Ryal or Royal " of Elizabeth, a twenty shilling piece of James I, a very fine five guinea piece of Charles II; several guineas of James II, William and Mary, Queen Anne, George I, also a quarter guinea of the same monarch, the first issue of this denomination in 1718; guineas and double guinea of George II and George III; also a " Spade guinea " of George III, so called from the shape of the shield on the reverse, which is very simple, and pointed like a spade, dated 1787; of George IV several half sovereigns, also two quarter sovereigns and several sovereigns; of this monarch there is also a fine five sovereign pattern; of William IV. sovereigns, half and quarter sovereigns; of Queen Victoria, several gold coins, among which the famous five pound piece, by Wyon, with the inimitable figure of Una and the Lion, which, though picturesque, is somewhat far-fetched, and little appropriate.

Among the British silver coins most prominent is the silver pound sterling, famous as the " siege piece " of Charles I, often made on the field of battle with hammer and anvil out of the family plate brought to the closely pressed, unhappy king by his followers. This siege piece is the largest silver coin known.

Several varieties of " Maundy money," also " Gun money " of James II; Scotch pennies, among which a very rare coin, the penny of Robert II of Scotland, said to be the only specimen in existence of that monarch's reign.

In this collection there are a number of English counter feits, prized because they are so well executed. Some of these give evidence of having been extensively circulated.

A handsome lot of English silver tokens, issued in England, Scotland and Ireland, make the British coin collection complete. These silver tokens were issued during the long

suspension of specie payments occasioned by the wars with
Napoleon. They were of reduced weight, to keep within the
premium and to prevent hoarding.

THE MEDAL CABINET OF THE MINT.

In 1859 the Hon. James Ross Snowden, Director of the
Mint, conceived the happy idea of collecting and placing in
the Cabinet of the National Mint, specimens of all the
medallic memorials of Washington. At that time he did not
know of the existence of more than twenty of such memorials; the Cabinet of the Mint contained only four or five
specimens. During an investigation, subsequently made, it
was ascertained that there were at least sixty different medals,
etc., of the above character.

The collection thus made was, therefore, arranged in an
appropriate case and formally inaugurated as a part of the
Cabinet of the Mint on the 22d day of February, 1860, on
which occasion a small medal known as the Washington,
Cabinet Memorial Medal was struck.

This medal has upon the obverse the bust of Washington,
facing to the right; legend, all around: "*GEORGE WASH-
INGTON *,BORN FEB. 22D 1732 * DIED DECEMBER 14 1799."
Reverse: A representation of the Washington Medallic Col-
lection, in the Cabinet of the Mint of the United States, sur-
mounted by a bust of Washington. Legend: "* WASHING-
TON CABINET OF MEDALS U. S. MINT *" L'Exergue: "INAU-
GURATED FEB. 22D 1860." Size 38.

The Mint also contains a monument to George Washing-
ton, composed of one hundred and fifty memorial medals.
Among this collection we notice the medal which was struck
at Paris in 1778, by direction of Voltaire. It bears upon the
obverse the head of Washington, facing to the right. Legend:
"G. WASHINGTON ER. GENERAL OF THE CONTIN'L ARMY IN
AMERICA." Reverse: Martial emblems, surrounded by
diverging rays. Legend: "WASHIN REUNIT PAR UN RARE
ASSEMBLAGE—LES TALENS DU GUERRIER & LES VERTUS
DU SAGE." Sixe 24.

• Only on two medals among the many we find Washington
represented as a warrior, and this was the first order of the
kind issued by the Continental Congress. The original medal
was of gold, and intended to commemorate the "Evacuation
of Boston, March 17th, 1776." The obverse bears the
undraped bust of Washington, facing to the right. Legend:

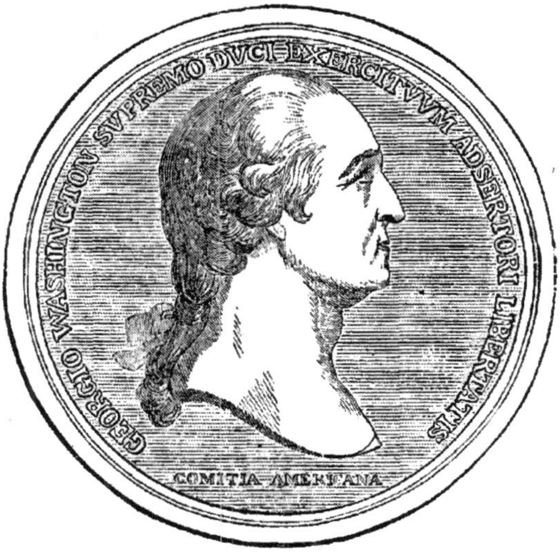
GEORGIO WASHINGTON SUPREMO DUCI EXERCITUUM ADSERTORI LIBERTATIS
COMITIA AMERICANA

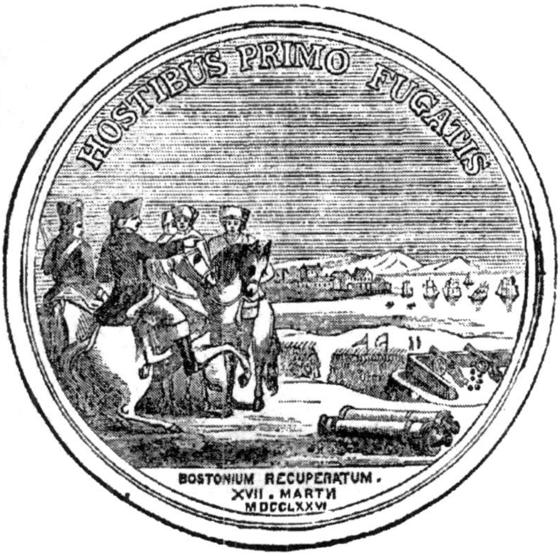
HOSTIBUS PRIMO FUGATIS
BOSTONIUM RECUPERATUM.
XVII. MARTII
MDCCLXXVI

39

"Georgio Washington Supremo Dvci Exercitrvm Adsertori Libertatis." Exergue : "Comitia Americana." Reverse : In the background appears the City of Boston, which the British troops are evacuating, and retiring to their shipping. To the right are the American intrenchments with the troops drawn up in front ready to march into the city. On an eminence in the left foreground is Washington and his staff mounted. Washington is pointing out the retiring enemy. on the ground are cannon and cannon balls. Legend : "Hostibus Primo Fugatis." Exergue: "Bostonium Recuperatum XVII Marti MDCCLXXVI." Size 42.

The largest Washington Medal was struck in iron and is just four and a fourth inches in diameter. It bears upon the obverse the bust of Washington, three quarter face, in citizen's dress. This medal has no legend and no reverse. It is generally admitted that this medal represents an excellent likeness of General Washington.

Another medal in this valuable collection, which has an excellent likeness of Washington is known as the large Mount Vernon medal. Upon the obverse, the bust of Washington, facing to the right. Legend: "George Washington." The whole is surrounded by an exquisite workmanship representing a circle composed of a number of hoops united with bands, emblematic of union and strength. Reverse: A representaton of Washington's residence at Mount Vernon, beneath which is inscribed, "Mount Vernon in 1796," and the name "J. Crutchett Mt. Vernon Factory." The whole inclosed by circle of hoops corresponding with the obverse. Size 50.

Of this Mount Vernon medal there is also one which has upon the reverse a representation of the Tomb of Washington at Mount Vernon.

In this Washington Medal Collection is the well-known "Silver Penny" of Washington. It bears upon the obverse the bust of Washington, in uniform, facing to the left. Beneath is the date 1792. Legend : "G. WASHINGTON PRESIDENT I." Reverse: An eagle, with raised wings; the U. S. shield upon its breast, an olive branch in the right and six arrows in the left talon. Around the edge are fifteen stars. Legend: "UNITED STATES OF AMERICA." Edge plain. Size 22.

Another and unique peice in this valuable collection is the one presented by H. Drumheller, of Schuylkill county, Pa. It bears upon the obverse the bust of Washington, surrounded

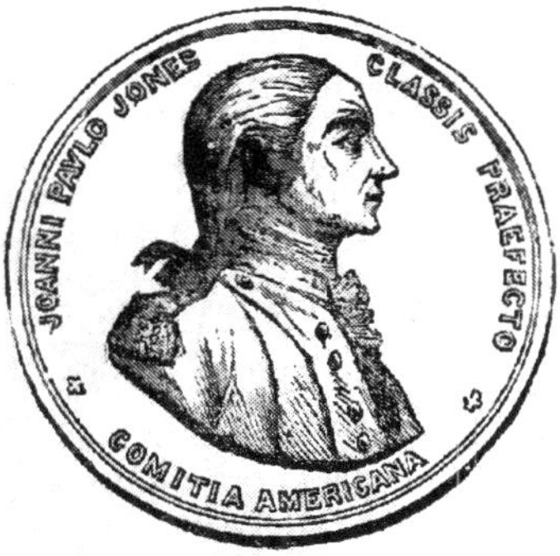
JOANNI PAVLO JONES
CLASSIS PRAEFECTO
COMITIA AMERICANA

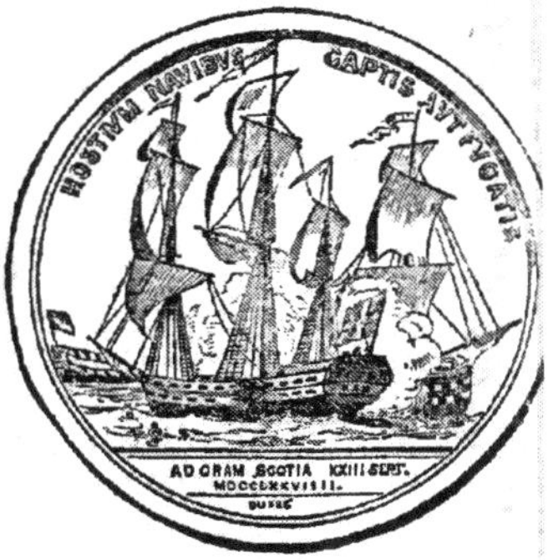
HOSTIVM NAVIBVS CAPTIS AVT FVGATIS
AD ORAM SCOTIA XXIII SEPT.

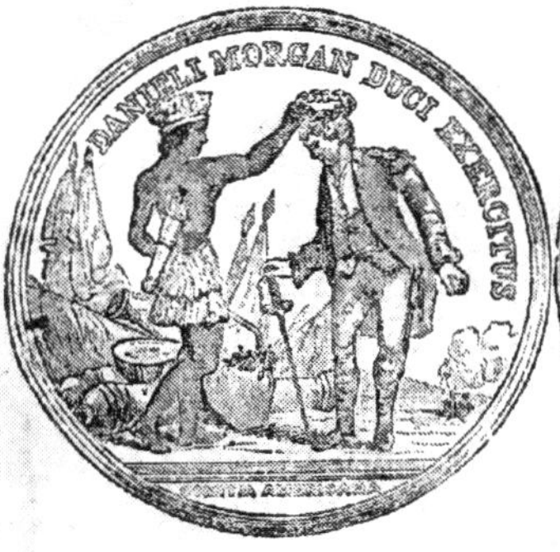
DANIELI MORGAN DUCI EXERCITUS

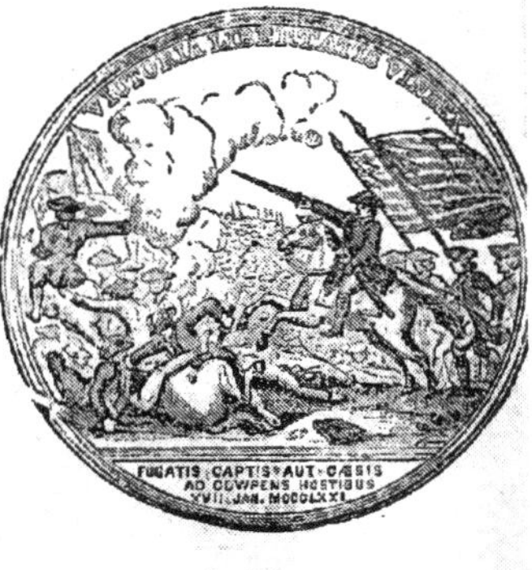
FUGATIS CAPTIS AUT CÆSIS
AD COWPENS HOSTIBUS

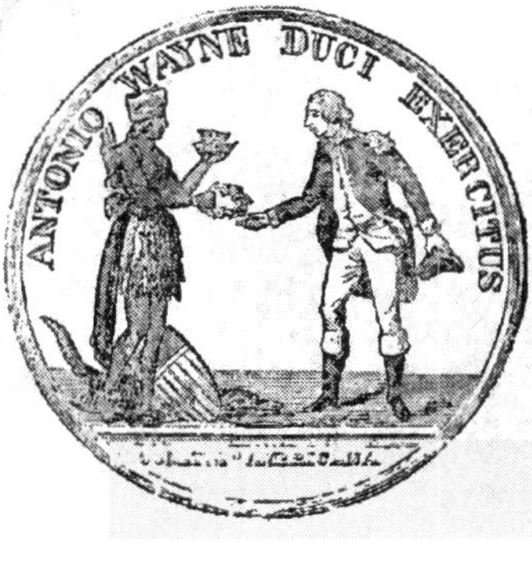
ANTONIO WAYNE DUCI EXERCITUS

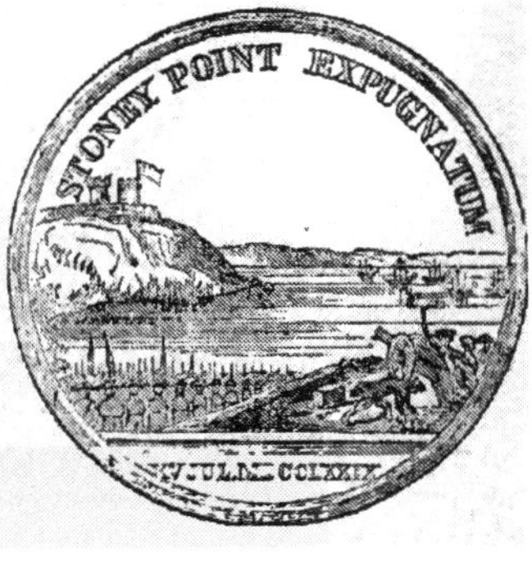
STONEY POINT EXPUGNATUM

Legend: " WASHINGTON PRESIDENT." Reverse: Eagle with raised wings, with fifteen stars above; in the left talon is an olive branch, and in the right six arrows; the legend: " UNITED STATES OF AMERICA," surrounded by rays of the sun running inside. Size 34.

In addition to the forgoing, the Washington Cabinet in the U.' S. Mint of Philadelphia contains many other memorials of Washington, Several medallions, badges, pens, breastpins and buttons, some of which have been used as badges, and worn by societies. Of the prominent badges there is a bust of Washington in brass; in this badge the outside metal has been cut away leaving the simple bust. There is also a gentlemen's breastpin bearing a small bust of Washington at three quarter face to the right; it is printed on paper and placed in small circular rim or cap, and covered with glass; beneath the cap containing the bust is attached a square and compass.

There is also a bust of Washington enveloped in a Roman mantle, and facing to the right, cut in lava from Mount Vesuvius.

A seal of the " Washington Lodge of Odd Fellows," Norfolk, Va., has also the bust of Washington.

There are also four Washington buttons in this Cabinet which were worn at the period of his presidency.

The U. S. Mint, then located on North Seventh street, in this city, was almost daily visited by Washington, and the following incident is well worthy to be recorded in this work.

General Washington, whose habit it was to see the heads of departments every week at his table, upon one of these occasions expressed to the Director of the Mint, the Hon. Henry William De Saussure,* his satisfaction at the activity which had been introduced into the silver coinage, and added, " I have long desired to see gold coined at the Mint, but your predecessor found insuperable difficulties. I should be much gratified if it could be accomplished before I leave office."

" I will try," was the reply; and Mr. De Saussure went to the Mint, summoned the private officers, ascertained the wants and difficulties of each department, and by great diligence, speedily removed all obstacles. In six weeks he carried to Washington a handful of gold " Eagles," and received his thanks and approbation.

* Mr. De Saussure was the Director of the Mint from the 11th day of July to the 28th of October, 1795; this incident, therefore, confirms the statement that the first coinage of gold at the U. S. Mint must have taken place in 1795.

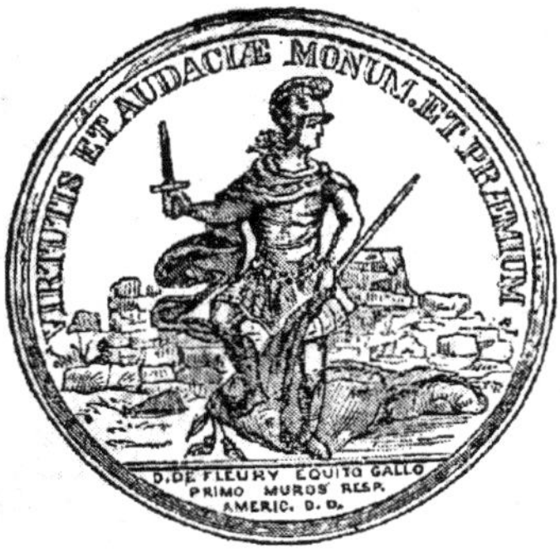
VIRTUTIS ET AUDACIÆ MONUM. ET PRÆMIUM
D. DE FLEURY EQUITO GALLO
PRIMO MUROS RESP.
AMERIC. D. D.

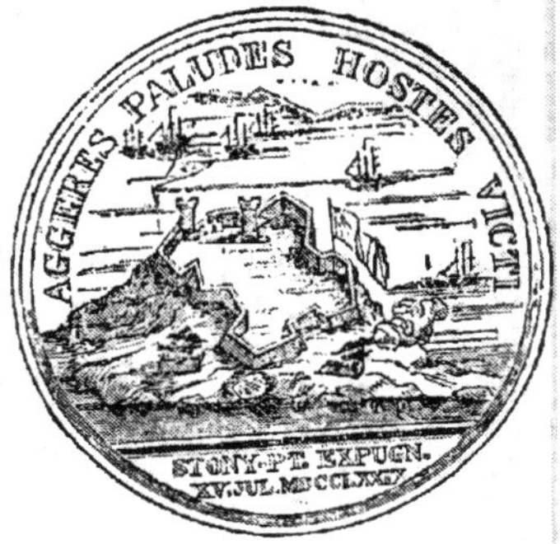
AGGERES PALUDES HOSTES VICTI
STONY-PT. EXPUGN.
XV. JUL. MDCCLXXIX

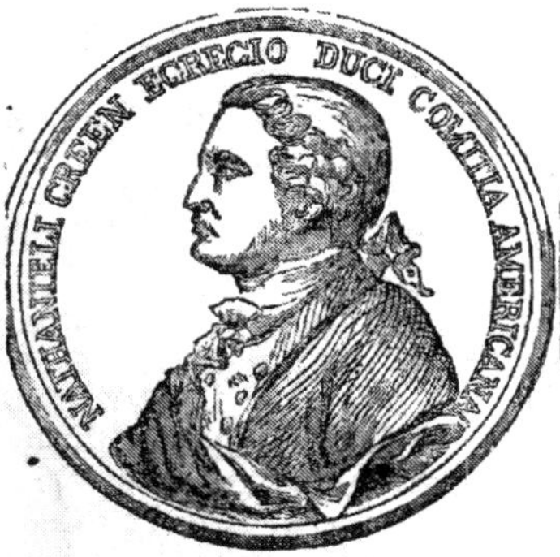
NATHANIELI CREEN ECRECIO DUCI COMITIA AMERICANA

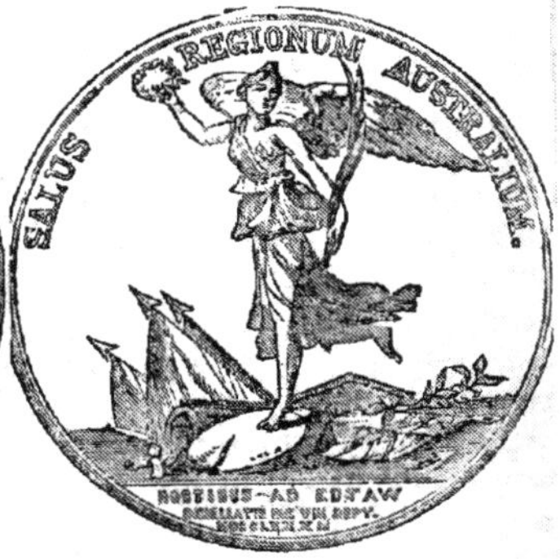
SALUS REGIONUM AUSTRALIUM.

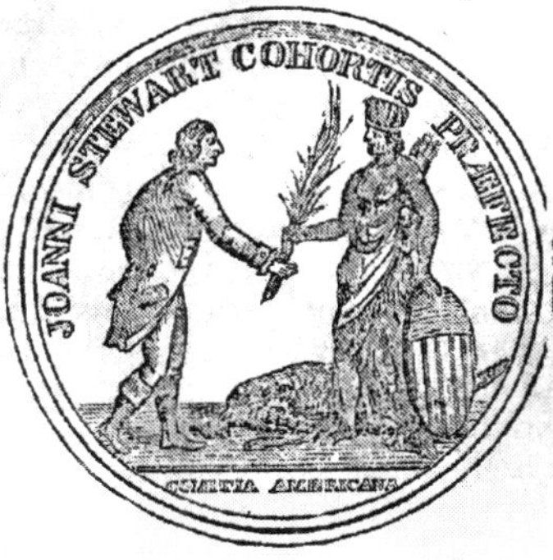
JOANNI STEWART COHORTIS PRÆFECTO
COMITIA AMERICANA

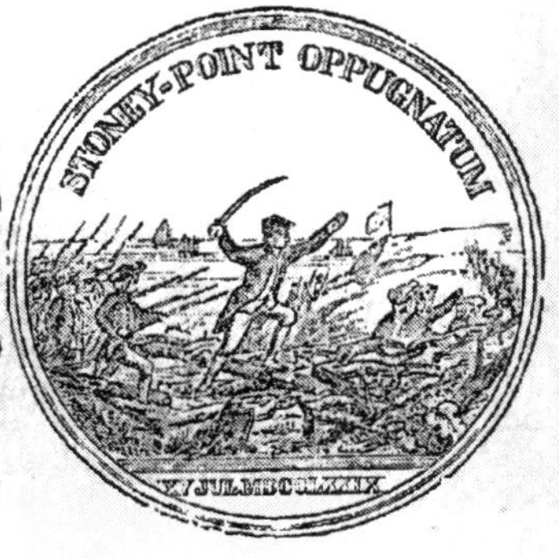
STONEY-POINT OPPUGNATUM
XV JUL. MDCCLXXIX

In the U. S. Mint Cabinet is also found an excellent and varied collection of National Medals, among which the Presidential Medals form a complete set. The army and navy of the U. S. is also well represented by its faithful officers and heroes. The miscellaneous medal collection is varied but of less national importance, although the medals of foreign governments are of the highest class of art.

· The "Washington before Boston" Medal is the only Washington Memorial struck by order of the U. S. Congress, and was struck in gold.

Of the Army of the Revolution, the following prominent medals must be recorded: Major-General Gates, Major General Wayne, Captain Stewart, Colonel Fleury, Major Henry Lee, General Morgan, Colonel John Egar Howard, Colonel William Washington, and Major-General Greene.

In this class of the Army of Revolution Medals are three silver medals which were awarded by vote of Congress of November 3d, 1780, to John Paulding, David Williams and Isaac Van Wert, who captured Major John Andre in the character of a spy, and notwithstanding the large bribes offered them for his release, secured and conveyed him to the commanding officer of the district, whereby the dangerous and traitorous conspiracy of Benedict Arnold was brought to light.

These medals were presented to the three heroes in the presence of the whole American army, in 1781, by General Washington, together with a copy of the resolution of Congress, awarding them each a pension of $200 annually during life, and a vote of thanks for their patriotic conduct.

These medals, of oblong shape, have upon the obverse, as device, a raised shield surrounded by branches of laurel and palm, and the legend: "FIDELITY." Reverse: A wreath formed of palm branches inclosing a blank for the insertion of the name of the recipient of the medal. Legend: "VINCIT AMOR PATRIAO." (*Love of patriotism conquers.*)

To Commerate the Triumph of American Independence.—Device: The bust of the Goddess of Liberty. The liberty pole surmounted by the cap, rest against the right shoulder, and the hair is blown back, as if by the wind against which the Goddess appears to be running to announce to the world the tidings of her victory. Legend: LIBERTAS AMERICANA 4 JUIL. 1776. Reverse: Pallas holding in her left hand a shield with three fleur de lis—the arms of France and opposing it to a leopard—England—which is springing towards it. Her right hand is drawn back and holding a barbed javelin

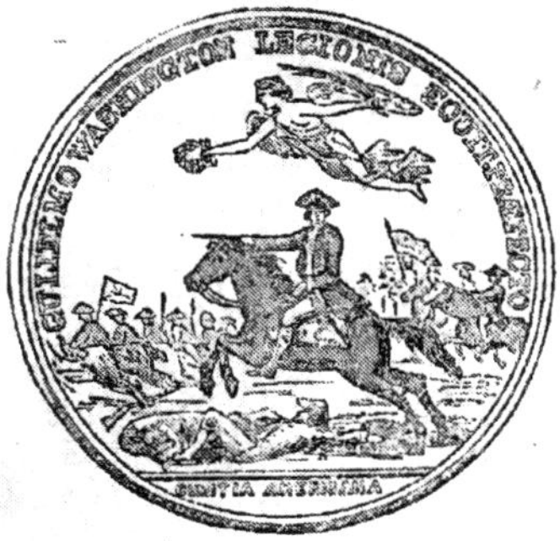
GULIELMO WASHINGTON LEGIONIS EQUIT. PRÆFECTO
COMITIA AMERICANA

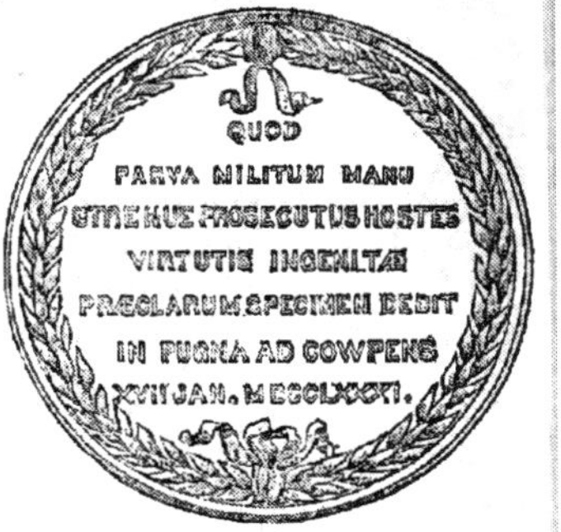
QUOD
PARVA MILITUM MANU
STRENUE PROSECUTUS HOSTES
VIRTUTIS INGENITÆ
PRÆCLARUM SPECIMEN DEDIT
IN PUGNA AD COWPENS
XVII JAN. MDCCLXXXI.

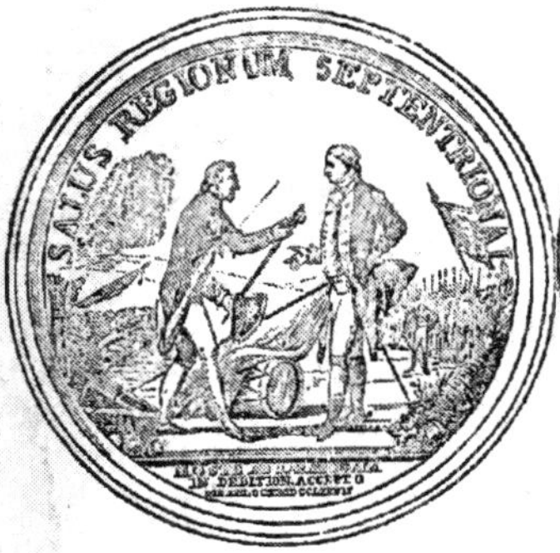
SALUS REGIONUM SEPTENTRIONAL

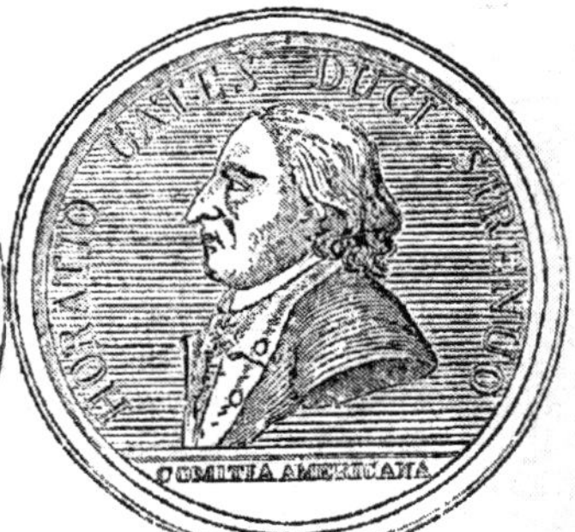
HORATIO GATES DUCI STRENUO
COMITIA AMERICANA

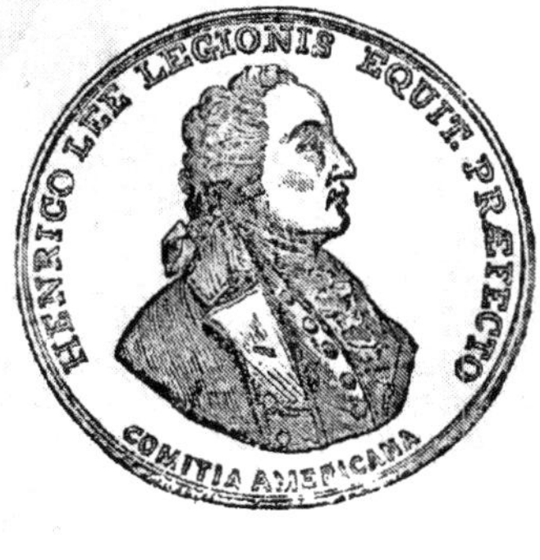
HENRICO LEE LEGIONIS EQUIT. PRÆFECTO
COMITIA AMERICANA

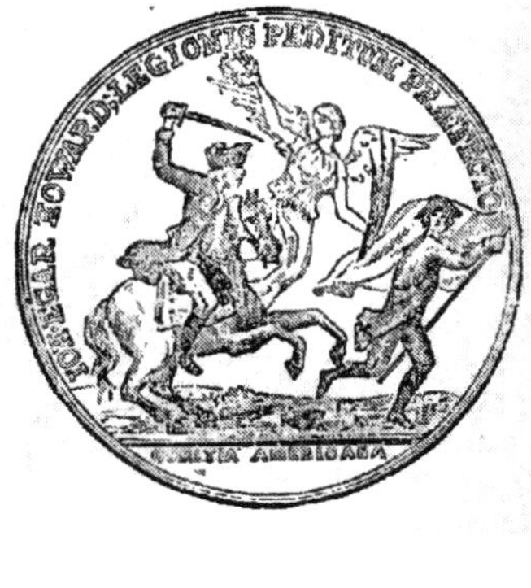
JOH. EGAR. HOWARD LEGIONIS PEDITUM PRÆFECTO
COMITIA AMERICANA

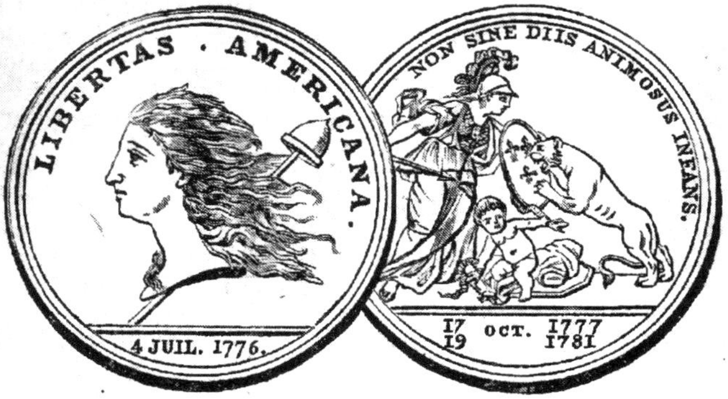
LIBERTAS . AMERICANA.
4 JUIL. 1776.
NON SINE DIIS ANIMOSUS INFANS.
17 OCT. 1777
19 1781

as if in the act of plunging it into the leopard. Under the shield is an infant in a stooping posture, strangling a serpent with each hand, and apparently contemplating the same act upon another at its feet. Legend: "NON SINE DIIS ANIMOSUS INFANS." Exergue: "Oct. 17, 1777, Oct. 19, 1781."

According to ancient mythology, Hercules, under the protection of Pallas is said to have strangled two serpents which had assaulted him in his cradle, Infant America, like Hercules in his cradle had destroyed two armies—Burgoyne's, which surrendered at Saratoga, Oct. 17, 1777, and Cornwallis, at Yorktown, Oct. 19, 1781.—From Mease's Description of American Medals.

The Wars of 1812—1815 have also been well remembered by medals struck in honor of its heroes. Among the prominent we find: Colonel George Croghan, Major-General Harrison, Governor Isaac Shelby, Major-General Scott, Major-General Gaines, Major-General Porter, Major-General Brown, Brigadier-General Miller, Brigadier-General Ripley, Major-General Macomb, and Major-General Jackson. This last medal of gold was awarded to General Jackson, by resolution of Congress of February 27, 1815, for his brave and successful repulse of the English troops, under General Sir Edward Packenham, in their attack upon New Orleans, January 8, 1815. This medal has upon the obverse the bust of General Jackson and the legend: "MAJOR GENERAL ANDREW JACKSON." The reverse bears as device: Victory seated, sustaining with her left hand, in which she holds a laurel wreath, and from which a palm branch has fallen, a tablet upon which she is about to note the victory of the 8th of January,

1815, heading the record with the name " ORLEANS." She is interrupted by Peace, bearing an olive branch in her right hand, and touching the tablet with her left, and is directing her to register the termination of the war between the United States and Great Britain, and the consummation of the peace consequent thereupon. Legend: " RESOLUTION OF CONGRESS FEBRUARY 27, 1815." Exergue: " BATTLE OF NEW ORLEANS, JANUARY 8, 1815." This medal is 2½ inches in diameter.

The war with Mexico is also well recorded by several medals, mostly of gold, of which three in honor of Major-General Taylor and one very large one in honor of Major-General Winfield Scott.

Our little difficulties with France are commemorated by a gold medal in honor of Captain Thomas Truxtun. The occasion for this medal was the action of the 2d of February, 1800, between the American frigate "Constellation," commanded by Captain Truxtun, and the French frigate "La Vengeance." The French were defeated. A gold medal was struck by order of Congress of March 24, 1800, to Captain Truxtun for his gallant behavior. The obverse of this medal bears the head of Captain Truxtun, but no legend. The reverse has a device, a representation of the engagement between the French frigate La Vengeance and the American frigate Constellation; both vessel are represented as much shattered and their rigging much cut. No legend. Exergue: " BY VOTE OF CONGRESS TO THOMAS TRUXTUN 24 MARCH, 1800."

The war with Tripoli is represented in this Cabinet collection by a gold medal to the gallant Commodore Preble for his bombardment of Tripoli on the 3d of August, 1804.

Among the many other medals in this Cabinet collection we must mention the " Wrecker's" and the "Shipwreck" medals, both of which are still struck occasionally. The Wrecker's medal has upon the obverse a mast, to which a man is clinging, floating in the sea; a ship is seen in the distance, the mast bears the letters " U. S." The reverse: A branch of oak and laurel crossed. The American Eagle and thirty-one stars. The centre of the space between the branches is left blank to receive the gallant recipient's name.

The shipwreck medal has as device upon the obverse a representation of a storm at sea; a lighthouse, and a sinking ship in the distance. A wrecker has just rescued and reached the shore with a person who has been shipwrecked. Above is a scroll to receive the recipient's name. Reverse: An eagle olive branch in his right, and a bunch of arrows in his left talon. Above the eagle's head is a scroll, bearing the words: "E Pluribus Unum," and in circle around the edge "United States of America."

These medals are struck for presentation to officers of vessels of foreign nations, as an acknowledgement of their services in saving the lives and property of shipwrecked Americans. The size of this medal is 2½ inches in diameter.

The Presidential Medals are series complete in themselves. The Washington medals as President of the U. S. are numerous, all bear his well-known effigy and appropriate inscriptions. Of President John Adams, unfortunately, there is only an unfinished medal. That die was never hardened, nor was there any reverse engraved for it either. Only a few copies were taken in soft metal.

Of Thomas Jefferson there are three medals; also three medals of each of the following presidents: James Madison, James Monroe, John Quincy Adams, Andrew Jackson, Martin Van Buren, John Tyler, James K. Polk and Zachary Taylor.

One medal of Millard Fillmore, Franklin Pierce and James Buchanan.

Of our martyr President Abraham Lincoln they are several very handsome medals. In these series we have especially to mention the grand "Emancipation Proclamation medal."

Andrew Johnson, U. S. Grant and Rutherford B. Hayes each have their appropriate medals and a place in that cabinet.

Before we can close the chapter on American Medals in the U. S. Cabinet Collection, we must call the attention of the visitors to the U. S. Mint, to the "Libertas Americana" medal, of which we reproduce an exact copy. (See page 45).

SUPERINTENDENT'S OFFICE.

On leaving the Coin Cabinet and prior to descending the marble steps, to the right is the office of the Superintendent of the Mint.

The present incumbent of this responsible office is the Hon. Archibald Loudon Snowden.

HON. ARCHIBALD LOUDON SNOWDEN,

who has been connected with the Mint service for nearly a
quarter of a century and is one of the representative men of
our City and State.

He was born in Cumberland County, Pa., and descends from
one of the oldest families in this State. His great ancestor
in America, William Fairfax Snowden, owned large tracts of
land in what was subsequently known as the "Old City proper," as early as 1669. His son John Snowden was born in
Philadelphia, August 1685, and was for many years one of
the most prominent merchants of the city, as were also his
son and grandson. The grandfather of Col. Snowden, the
Rev. Nathaniel Randolph Snowden, was born in Philadelphia
in 1770, and his father, Dr. Isaac Wayne Snowden, in 1790.
Dr. Snowden graduated at an early age in Medicine and
entered the military service under General Jackson as sur-
geon. He was with him at the battle of New Orleans and in
the Seminole War. At the close of the Florida campaign—
in which he was severely wounded—Dr. Snowden resigned
from the army and settled in the rich valley of the Cumberland, nine miles below Carlisle, Pa., where he practised his
profession with great success until his death in 1850. Shortly
after removing to Cumberland County he married the daugh-
ter of Archibald Loudon, Esq., one of the largest land owners
in that portion of this State; and from this union the subject
of our present sketch was born.

At a very early age, Col. Snowden was sent to an academy
and subsequently entered Jefferson, now Washington and
Jefferson College, in Washington, Pa. Here he received a
thorough education, and was particularly distinguished during
his collegiate course as the most brilliant and effective orator
in the College. He was twice selected by the Literary Society,
of which he was a member, as class orator. On the completion
of his collegiate course he began the study of law and shortly
after, on May 7th 1857, accepted the position of Register tendered him by his uncle the late Hon. James Ross Snowden,

---

hen Director of the U. S. Mint. Here his active mind, not satisfied with the simple discharge of the duties of his new position, sought constant employment both in and out of the Mint. Out of the Mint he continued the study of law, and cultivated literature; and was for several years President of the principal Literary Society of the city. In the Mint he voluntarily assumed and discharged duties which by right, belonged to three other gentlemen, who were performing work in the Sub-Treasury, then located in the Mint building, and which was overcrowded with business. All the duties devolving upon these different and responsible positions he faithfully discharged in addition to his duties as Register. In this indefatigable manner he continued to enlarge his sphere of usefulness, rendering the most valuable and acceptable services, and commanding at all times the confidence and esteem of his superior officers.

In 1866, a vacancy having occured in the office of Chief Coiner of the Mint, he was appointed by the President and unanimously confirmed by the Senate. For this place he received also the unanimous endorsement of all the officers of the Mint and of every Bank and Banker of this City. He entered upon the duties of this office October 1st 1866.

As Chief Coiner of the Mint, he was enabled to put into practical use the valuable information which he had been diligently acquiring for many years, and also had an opportunity for the exercise of his remarkable power of thorough organization, for which he is so justly distinguished. The coining department soon felt the impulse of his active and earnest spirit, and the most gratifying results followed. His successor in this important post freely admits that the thorough discipline, and the ingenious and rigid checks he introduced, are still the leading features of that department.

Within a brief period after entering this department, he completely revolutionized and reorganized it. Abuses of many years standing were corrected and reforms and economies introduced. He suggested and invented new and improved machinery, introduced new appliances, notably in connection with the coining and cutting presses and milling machines. He introduced from Vienna, Austria, the Seys Automatic Assorting Machine, which has worked a complete revolution in the separation of the planchets before coinage. He also had the Hill Reducing Machine imported from London, with its marvelous capabilities in the production of coinage and medal dies. In fact he introduced all the new appliances in coinage from the different countries and applied original ideas and inventions, until the department was brought to the highest standard of efficiency. Whilst thus prosecuting with great ardor and enthusiasm the delicate and important work entrusted to his care, he was suddenly and unexpectedly called upon to lay aside his agreeable and congenial duties and accept, at the request of President Grant, the Postmastership of Philadelphia, to which he had been nominated and unanimously confirmed by the Senate.

He assumed the new and untried duties with much reluctance, but soon manifested as Post Master the same capacity for thorough discipline and organization, which had distinguished him in the Mint. In his brief administration of the postal service of the city he gained credit for himself and rendered a most acceptable service to the public.

He introduced into the administration of the Post Office the same rules for its government that he had always observed in the Mint. His rule as to appointments and removals is simple, but very effective, namely: "All employees who do their duty will be retained, those who do not will be removed."

This rule was universal in its application, and no outside influence was permited to interfere with its operation. The humblest employee, without a friend, was as secure in his place, provided he did his duty, as if he had all the political influence of the State at his command.

Intoxication and tipling among the employees was stopped; courteous attention to duty became the rule, and the public received the best service possible, because it was intelligently and cheerfully given.

The general sentiment of the public was that Col. Snowden's stay in the Post Office would be brief, as his long service in the Mint demanded his return in that department.

This feeling was more keenly felt in the Treasury Department at Washington than elsewhere, and it was therefore a matter of no surprise when President Hayes in December, 1878, voluntarily tendered to him the position of Director of all the Mints, made vacant by the expiration of the commission of Dr. Linderman. After the death of Dr. Linderman, the President again sent for him and urged his acceptance of the place, which he was believed to have declined previous to Dr. Linderman's death from motives of delicacy having long been the friend of the late Director.

This tempting and very complimentary offer he again de-

clined, giving as his reason that its acceptance would necessi-
tate his removal from Philadelphia to Washington. It was
undoubtedly a severe trial, as the President coud have offered
him no place so entirely in harmony with his tasts and ambi-
tion.

Attachment for Philadelphia was stronger than his desire
to be at the head of a service which he had entered as a
youth nearly a quarter of a century before.

In the following February the President again made a vol-
untary tender of office, this time it was the Directorship of
the Philadelphia Mint, and as its acceptance restored him
once more to a service agreeable in every particular, and permitted him to remain among his friends in Philadelphia, he
promptly accepted, was agatn unanimously cofirmed by the
Senate, and assumed control of the Mint on the first of March,
1879.

His appointment to this honorable and responsible position
was universally recognized as placing "the right man in the
right place," and received the unqualified approval of the
press and public at large, without distinction of party.

Among those who are familiar with Mint affairs Col. Snowden is acknowledge to be, perhaps, the best informed man in
our country in all that relates to the history of coinage in general and to the coinage of the United States in particular. He
is thoroughly familiar with the establishment of our Mint system, with its gradual development and steady improvement;
knows all about its written and unwritten history, and is
thoroughly master of the theory and practical operations o
coinage.

Outside of his official life, he has always taken a deep
interest and most active part in the general current of events.

On the outbreak of the Rebellion he promptly offered his
services, and under authority from the Governor assisted in
enlisting and organizing a regiment which he offered to the
State. Declining the Colonelcy in favor of one who had much
experience and long service abroad; he was elected and commissioned Lieutenant-Colonel. The most solemn promises to
muster the Regiment into the service were overlooked or disre-
garded, until from the long delay and the expense of maintain-
ing the command intact, four of the companies tendered their
services to New York, and were incorporated into the Excelsior
Brigade commanded by General Sickles. The other six companies were ultimately sent into camp Washington at Easton,
Pa., but by an ingenious system of gerrymandering were so

52

divided among the other companies from different parts of
the State, that, although voting for their old field officers, their
voters in each Regiment to which they were assigned was not
a majority. Thus after months of labor and expense in enlisting, subsisting and clothing the men, the field officers were
by a contemptible trick deprived of the places to which they
were justly entitled.

On his return from Camp Washington, he was invited and
consented to resume his old place in the Mint. The disappoint-
ment he experienced in his military aspirations cannot but be
considered as a fortunate circumstance, in view of the
valuable and acceptable service he has since rendered to
the government and people in the important department
with which he has been so long identified. For many
years he was an active member of the First City Troop
and participated with it in the valuable service it rendered
during the late war, and ultimately became its Captain. For
many years he has taken an intelligent and active interest in
Railroad and Insurance matters. In January, 1873, he was
elected Vice President of the Fire Association, one of the
oldest, largest and soundest insurance companies in the
United States. In 1878 he was elected President of that
Company, and last year was elected President of the " United
Fire Underwriters of America," an organization embracing
the officers of more than one hundred and fifty of the leading
American and foreign companies doing business in the United
States, representing a capital and assets of over $118,000,000.

In the midst of the large demands made upon him by business and social interests, he finds time to cultivate his fine
literary taste, and within the past two or three years has delivered several notable addresses on scientific and other sub-
jects. His address before the literary societies of his old *Alma
Mater* on the " Achievement of man " was one the most
striking literary productions of the day, as was also his
address on *Bi-Metalism* before the Banker's Convention at
Saratoga in the summer of 1880.

His cogent arguments, sustained by historical and logical
illustration, produced a decided impression on the public
mind. The address, besides having a wide newspaper circulation, was printed in pamphlet form, and many thousands were
scattered throughout this country and abroad. Subsequent
events have singularly verified the views expressed therein, and
the failure of the Paris Monetary Convention to establish a fixed
ratio between gold and silver goes far toward vindicating the

opinion he boldly expressed on that occasion, to wit, that "the attempt to establish and successfully maintain a *Dual Standard* in the United States without the concurrent action of the intelligent commercial nations of the earth must prove a disastrous failure, and such concurrent action in my judgment, can not at present be had." He advised Congress to retrace its steps and place our legislation in harmony with that of the intelligent nations, who are free to act wisely, rather than continue a course which the longer it is followed will the more surely bring great injury upon our country.

His address at Chester upon the "Character of our government and the relation it sustains to all classes," and the subsequent one at Media, on "The duties imposed by American Citizenship," were both strikingly happy and full of valuable suggestions and patriotic utterances.

Among the many interesting and able addresses delivered on the occasion of the Celebration of the Centennial Anniversary of the Incorporation of "The American Philosophical Society of Philadelphia," which was founded by Benjamin Franklin, in 1743, and Incorporated March 15th, 1780, the one made by Col. Snowden on "The Need of an Elevated and Permanent Civil Service," was conspicuous for its lucid and practical presentation of a subject which is now commanding the attention of the country, and which is receiving the cordial support of some of our ablest and purest citizens.

His remarks on the occasion of the memorial service at Milford, Del., to his friend General Torbert, who perished with the ill-fated steamship *Vera Cruz*, were touchingly beautiful and appropriate, and stamped him as possessing the highest qualities of the impassioned orator. His speech in November, 1880, in the American Academy of Music in Philadelphia, before the manufacturers and laboring men of the city on the protection of American Industry, under the auspices of the Union League, was as brilliant as it was convincing. In this address he gave the history of protection in general, and particularly as effected by legislation in our own country, tracing it from the first message of Washington to the last attempt to overthrow the system.

In it he briefly touched upon the life and services of General Garfield, and referred to his long and heroic struggle with adversity, his steady but sure advancement to prominence, his high qualities of mind and heart, which the people were daily learning to appreciate, and predicted for him a grand future among the statesmen of America and an abiding place in the hearts of his countrymen.

The eulogy pronounced then, if read now in the light of recent events, and in view of the heroic bearing and noble qualities of that illustrious man, as exhibited in his protracted sufferings, would be endorsed by all America without distinction of class or party.

As a post-prandial speaker he is brilliant, entertaining and instructive, and is always welcomed as one who can be relied upon, with or without notice, to meet the highest expectation of an occasion.

It will thus be seen that the subject of our sketch is many sided, and that, whilst giving the closest and most conscientious attention to the duties that officially devolve upon him, at the same time takes a deep personal interest and active part in all that affects the general welfare.

Of him it can be truthfully said, that in the important positions of trust and responsibility which he has held, he has at all times manifested the highest intelligence, the most untiring energy and thorough integrity.

He is proverbially polite and obliging to all who have business intercourse with him, and takes pleasure in imparting information when in his power to bestow it.

This courtesy united with his other genial qualities has made him a host of friends in all the walks of life.

In his public and private life he commands the confidence of the Government he has so long and faithfully served, and the respect and esteem of the public at large.

THE COINING DEPARTMENT.

Descending the marble steps leading from the floor of the Cabinet to the first story, on the left is the department of the Coiner.

The present Coiner of the Mint is Colonel Oliver Christian Bosbyshell. This gentleman was born in Vicksburg, Miss., January 3, 1839, where his parents had temporarily settled. His father, Oliver C. Bosbyshell, and his mother Mary A. Whitney, were born in Philadelphia, and their ancestors, for many generations back were also Philadelphians. His father dying a month or two before the subject of this sketch was born, his mother returned to Pennsylvania, and found a home with her father Lebbens Whitney, in Schuylkill County. In this County Col. Bosbyshell was reared and educated. At fifteen he left the public school, with a fair education, to take the position of telegraph messenger in the office of the Philadelphia and Reading Railroad Telegraph Company, in Pottsville. For three years he was employed as messenger and operator, when he went into the law office of Hon. F. W. Hughes, as clerk, intending to devote his attention to the law. Two years later he entered the law office of his uncle, Wm. L. Whitney, Esq., as a regular student, and was thus engaged when the Rebellion broke out. In response to President Lincoln's proclamation for volunteers, he entered Washington, D. C., on the 18th of April 1861, as a private, in the now historic Washington Artillerists of Pottsville, Pa., one of the first Companies to reach the Capitol of the Nation. During this three months service he was tendered a commission in the regular army, which he declined. Upon the formation of the 48th Regiment Pennsylvania Volunteers, for three years, in September, 1861, he was commissioned Second Lieutenant of Company "G" by Governor Curtin, being the junior office in the regiment. His service during the war was honorable to himself, and creditable to his State. By successive promotion, to 1st. Lieutenant and Captain, he finally became Major of the Regiment.

After the close of the war he engaged in business in Pottsville, Pa. He has always taken a lively interest in the welfare of the soldier, is a prominent member of the Grand Army of the Republic, having commanded the Department of Pennsylvania in 1869, and continually identified since in every movement for the welfare of that organization.. He is also a member of the National Guard of the State, being Lieutenant-Colonel of the Second Regiment of Philadelphia.

Colonel Bosbyshell's connection with the United States Mint began on the 4th of May, 1869, when Ex-Governor Pollock then Director, appointed him Register of Deposits. His course in the Mint was so satisfactory, that, without solicitation, he was made Assistant Coiner by Col. A. L. Snowden, the then Coiner, on the 1st of October, 1872. Upon Colonel Snowden's appointment as Postmaster of Philadelphia, Colonel Bosbyshell, was appointed Coiner of the Mint, by President Grant, on the 15th of December. 1876.

In his connection with the Mint, both as Assistant to the Coiner, and as Coiner, Colonel Bosbyshell has brought to bear in the discharge of his duties all that rare executive ability, and scrupulous fidelity to his trust, for which he was distinguished in the military service, his uniform kindness and consideration toward the many employed in his department, has secured for him the respect and esteem of his subordinates, while his courteous bearing in his intercourse with the officers and clerks of other departments, has won for him the respect and lasting friendship of all. It is through the probity and courtesy of such officers as Colonel Bosbyshell, that the civil service of a country must be elevated and popularized, if at all.

UNITED STATES COINS.

Gold Coins.

Double Eagles.—Authorized to be coined by Act of March 3, 1849. Weight, 516 grains, and 900 fine.

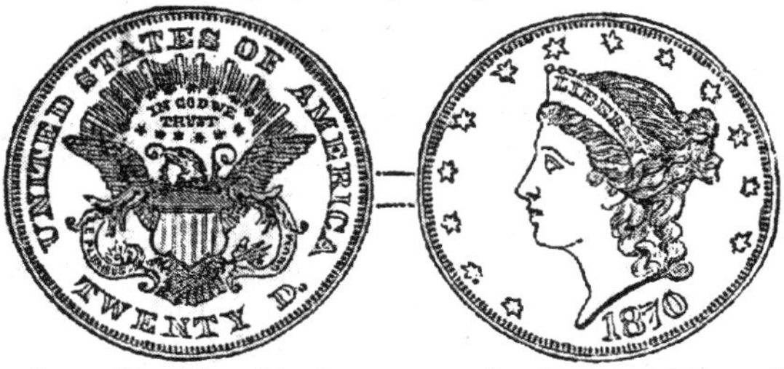
UNITED STATES OF AMERICA
IN GOD WE TRUST
TWENTY D.
LIBERTY
1870

The first Double Eagle was coined in 1849. It has upon the obverse the head of Liberty, facing to the left, hair tied behind, a coronet upon the forehead, on which: "Liberty." Thirteen stars and date. Upon the reverse: An eagle, with shield upon its breast, an olive branch and three arrows in its talons; in its beak an elaborate scroll, upon which, "E Pluribus Unum." Above, a circle of thirteen stars and a curved line of rays extending from wing to wing. "United States of America." "Twenty D." This coinage, bearing the above obverses and reverses, was continued up to 1865, inclusive. In 1866 the words "In God we trust" was inscribed within the circle of stars on the reverse; and continued up to 1876, inclusive. In 1877, and up to the present time, all the above mentioned impressions were continued, and, instead of "Twenty D." upon the reverse, the change was made to read, "Twenty Dollars."

Eagles.—Authorized to be coined by Act of April 2, 1792. Weight, 270 grains, and 916.66 fine. By Act of June 28, 1834, the weight was changed to 258 grains, and the fineness to 899.225. Again, by Act of January 18, 1837, the fineness was changed to 900 fine, and remains the same up to the present time.

The first coinage of Eagles took place in 1795. Upon the obverse is the head of "Liberty," wearing a cap, facing to the right. Fifteen stars. Above is inscribed: "Liberty,"

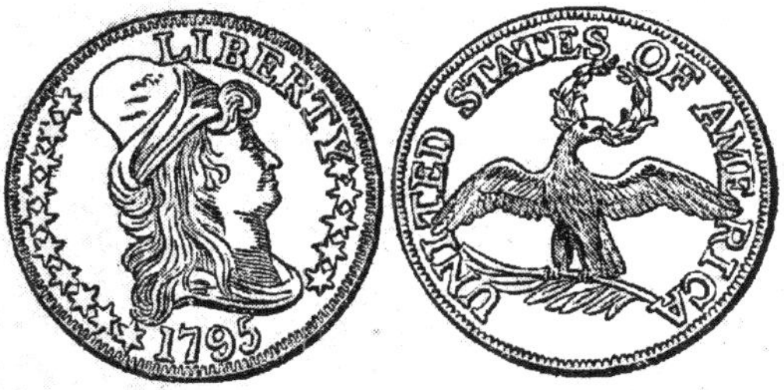
LIBERTY
1795
UNITED STATES OF AMERICA

and below the date of the year of issue. Upon the reverse: An eagle, with extended wings, standing upon a palm branch, holding in his beak a laurel wreath: "United States of America," In 1796 no change was made in the device, only the fifteen stars on the obverse were replaced by sixteen stars. This was done on the occasion of the admission of Tennessee into the Union as the sixteenth State. This system of the adornment of our coinage was commenced in 1796, but continued for a short time only.

In 1797 there were coined two varieties of Eagles; the first coinage was the same as that of the preceding year; the second was similar so far as the obverse is concerned, but the reverse was changed. The reverse bears an eagle with the U. S. shield upon its breast, a bundle of arrows in the right talon, and an olive branch in the left; in its beak a scroll, inscribed: "E Pluribus Unum." Around the head are thirteen stars, above a curved line of clouds extending from wing to wing. "United States of America."

During 1798, 1799, 1800 and 1801 the same devices of the second coinage of 1797 were continued.

In 1802 none were issued.

In 1803 and 1804 the same devices of 1801 were continued.

From 1805 to 1837, inclusive, none were issued.

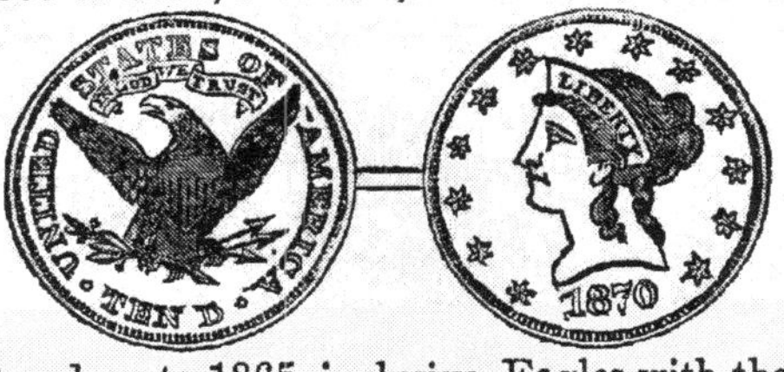
UNITED STATES OF AMERICA
IN GOD WE TRUST
TEN D.
LIBERTY
1870

In 1838 and up to 1865, inclusive, Eagles with the following devices were coined: Obverse, head of Liberty, facing to the left, hair tied behind, a coronet upon the forehead, on which is inscribed: "Liberty." Above thirteen stars. Upon the reverse: Eagle, with the U. S. shield upon its breast, and an olive branch and three arrows in the talon. "United States of America." "Ten D."

In 1866, and up to the present time, the same devices as those of 1838—1865 were continued, with the addition of the motto: "In God we trust."

Half-Eagles.—Authorized to be coined by Act of April 2, 1792. Weight, 135 grains, and 916.666 fineness. This weight was changed, by Act of June 28, 1834, to 129 grains, and the fineness to 899.225 fine: further, by Act of January 18, 1837, the fineness was changed to 900 fine, and has remained in that fineness and weight to the present time.

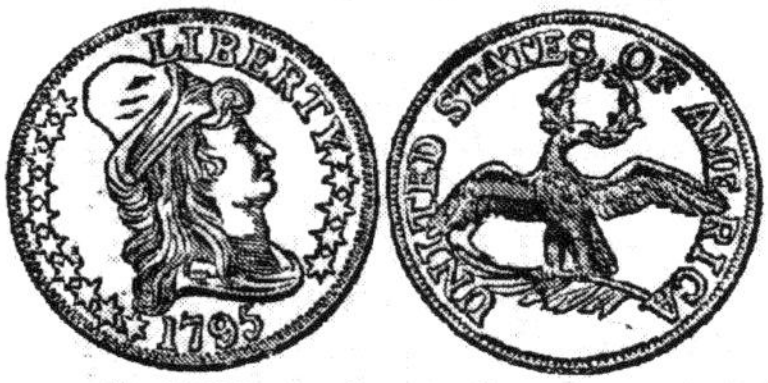
LIBERTY
1795
UNITED STATES OF AMERICA

The coinage of 1795, when the first Half-Eagles were struck, bears upon the obverse: Head of Liberty, wearing a cap, facing to the right. Fifteen stars. Above "Liberty." Reverse: Eagle with extended wings, standing upon a palm branch, holding in his beak a laurel wreath. "United States of America."

The second coinage of 1795 bears the same obverse as the first, but the reverse was changed. It bears an eagle with the U. S. shield upon its breast, a bundle of arrows in the left, in its beak a scroll upon which is inscribed "E Pluribus Unum." Around the head are thirteen stars; above is a curved line of clouds extending from wing to wing. "United States of America.

In 1796 the same devices as those of the second coinage of 1795 were continued.

The Half-Eagles of the coinage of 1797 include three distinct types. The first coinage of 1797 is similar in every particular to the coinage of 1796. The second coinage of that year is also similar to that of the first of this year, the only differences are 16 stars on the obverse. The third coinage was struck from an altered die of the second coinage of 1795 and has the same devices with the exception of the date of the year of issue.

The coinages of 1798 are two-fold. The first bears upon the obverse: Head of Liberty wearing a cap, facing to the right; above "Liberty." Reverse: Eagle with extended wings, standing upon a palm branch, holding in his beak a laurel wreath. "United States of America."

The second coinage of 1798 has the same obverse as the first, but the reverse has an eagle, a U. S. shield upon its breast, in his talons bundle of arrows and an olive branch, in its beak a scroll upon which is inscribed "E Pluribus Unum," around the head are thirteen stars and above is a curved line of clouds extending from wing to wing, also the legend "United States of America."

During 1799 and 1800 the Half-Eagles were coined with similar devices of the second coinage of 1798, with change of date of the year of issue.

In 1801 no Half-Eagles were issued.

In 1802, 1803, 1804, 1805, and 1806, the coinages respectively bear the following devices: Head of Liberty wearing a cap, facing to the right; above "Liberty." Reverse: An eagle with a U. S. shield upon its breast, in his talons bundle of arrows and an olive branch, in its beak a scroll upon which is inscribed "E Pluribus Unum" around the head are thirteen stars and above is a curved line of clouds extending from wing to wing and the legend "United States of America."

LIBERTY
1807
STATES OF
E PLURIBUS UNUM
UNITED
AMERICA

In 1807 there were again two distinct coinages. The first coinage has upon the obverse: Head of Liberty wearing a cap, facing to the right. Above "Liberty" and below the date of issue. Reverse: An eagle with a U. S. shield upon its breast, a bundle of arrows in the right talon and an olive branch in the left, in its beak a scroll upon which is inscribed "E Pluribus Unum." Around the head are thirteen stars, above is a curved line of clouds extending from wing to wing. "United States of America." The second coinage has upon the obverse: Liberty head facing to the left, bust draped, wearing a kind of turban with a band in front, inscribed "Liberty." Thirteen stars and date. Reverse: An eagle with U. S. shield upon its breast, an olive branch and three arrows in the talons; above a scroll inscribed "E Pluribus Unum," "United States of America," and below the head "5 D."

During 1808, 1809, 1810, 1811 and 1812 there was but one coinage each year, preserving the same devices as upon the Half-Eagle of the second coinage of 1807, the die being only altered to change the date of the year of issue.

During 1813, 1814 and 1815, there was again only one coinage each year, but the dies were somewhat altered. Upon the obverse they have the head of Liberty, facing to the left, wearing a kind of turban, a band in front, upon which is inscribed "Liberty," around are thirteen stars, below the date of the year of issue. Reverse: An eagle with U. S. shield upon its breast, an olive branch and three arrows in the talons; above a scroll inscribed "E Pluribus Unum," and "United States of America" as legend; below, as exergue, "5 D." During the years 1816 and 1817 no Half-Eagles were issued.

In 1818, and up to 1828 inclusive, the Half-Eagles bear upon the obverse: Liberty head, facing to the left, wearing a turban, upon the band of which is inscribed "Liberty;" around are thirteen stars, below the date of each respective year of issue. Reverse: An eagle with U. S. shield upon its breast, an olive branch and three arrows in the talons; above, a scroll with "E Pluribus Unum," and as legend "United States of America." As exergue: "Five D."

In 1829 there were two distinct coinages of Half-Eagles; they were both similar to the issue of 1818-1828, but the size of coin of the coinage was reduced one-sixteenth of an inch in diameter.

In 1830, and up to 1833, inclusive, the Half-Eagle bear the same devices as those of 1829, but their size corresponds with the reduction of the second coinage of 1829.

In 1834 there were again two distinct coinages. The first bears upon the obverse Head of Liberty, facing to the left, wearing a turban, upon the band of which is inscribed "Liberty;" around are thirteen stars, below the date of the year of issue. Reverse: An eagle with U. S. shield upon its breast, an olive branch and three arrows in the talons, above a scroll with "E Pluribus Unum;" legend: "United States of America;" exergue: "Five D."

The second coinage has upon the obverse Liberty head, facing to the left, the hair confined by a band, upon which is inscribed "Liberty." Reverse: An eagle with U. S. shield upon its breast, an olive branch and three arrows in the talons; legend: "United States of America;" exergue: "Five D." In this year's second coinage the size of the Half-Eagle was again reduced by one-sixteenth of an inch.

In 1835, and up to 1838, inclusive, the devices and size were preserved and conformed with the second coinage of 1834.

In 1839 an entire new die was prepared. It bears upon the obverse Head of Liberty to the left, hair tied behind by strings of beads, around the forehead a plain coronet, upon which is inscribed "Liberty;" around are thirteen stars, and as exergue "1839." Reverse: An eagle with wings displayed upwards, on his breast the U. S. shield, in his talons an olive branch and three arrows; as legend: "United States of America," and as exergue "Five D."

In 1840, and up to 1865, no change was made in the devices, the die being only altered each year to the date of issue.

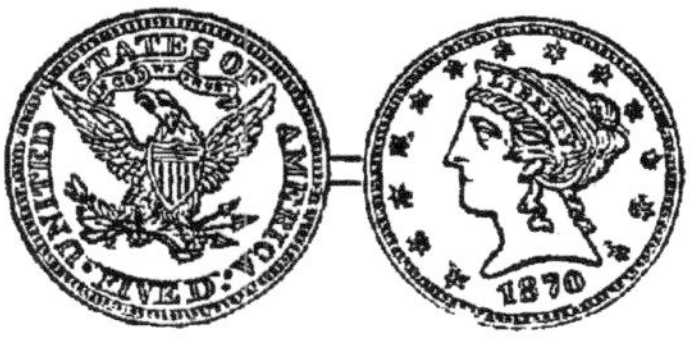
UNITED STATES OF AMERICA
FIVE D.
LIBERTY
1870

1866 a change was made. Upon the obverse: Liberty head, facing to the left, hair tied behind, a coronet upon the forehead, upon which is inscribed "Liberty;" thirteen stars, and as exergue the date of the year of issue. Upon the reverse an eagle with U. S. shield upon its breast, an olive branch and three stars in the talons. As legend: "United States of America;" as exergue: "Five D." Above the eagle appears for the first time the motto: "In God we trust."

In 1867, and up to the present time, no change was made in the devices, and the dies were only altered in conformity of the date of each year of issue.

Quarter-Eagles.—The Quarter-Eagles were authorized to be coined by Act of Congress, April 2, 1792. Their original weight was 67½ grains, and their fineness 916.666. Their weight and fineness was changed by Act of June 28, 1834, to 64½ grains, and their fineness to 899.225 fine. This latter one was again changed January 18, 1837, to 900 fine, and has remained so ever since.

The first issue of Quarter-Eagles took place in 1796. In that year there were two distinct coinages, one having sixteen stars on the obverse, the other without stars. Upon the obverse is the head of Liberty, facing to right, above "Liberty" and sixteen stars. Reverse: An eagle with the U. S. shield upon its breast, a bundle of arrows in its right talon and an olive branch in the left: in its beak a scroll, upon which is inscribed: "E Pluribus Unum." Around the head are thirteen stars, above a curved line of clouds, extending from wing to wing, "United States of America."

In 1797 and 1798 a slight alteration was again made, Obverse: Head of Liberty, above the word "Liberty" thirteen stars. Reverse: an eagle, from its beak a scroll with "E Pluribus Unum" upon the same; around the head are thirteen stars surrounded by clouds, the whole encircled by the words, "United States of America."

During 1799, 1800 and 1801 no Quarter-Eagles were issued.

In 1802 the coinage of Quarter-Eagles was resumed. They bear upon the obverse head of Liberty, facing to the right, above the same "Liberty" and thirteen stars. Reverse: An eagle with the U. S. shield upon its breast, a bundle of arrows in the right talon and an olive branch in the left; in the beak a scroll. upon which: "E Pluribus Unum;" around the head are thirteen stars above a curved line of clouds, extending from wing to wing, surrounded by the words "United States of America."

In 1803 no Quarter-Eagles were issued.

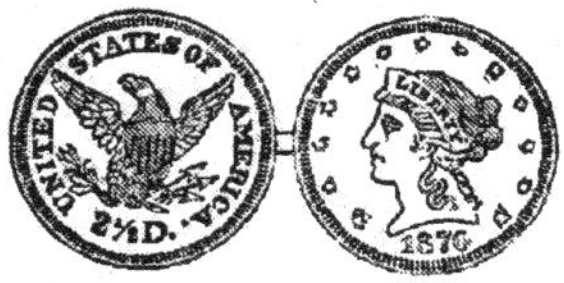
UNITED STATES OF AMERICA
2½D.
LIBERTY
1876

In 1804, 1805, 1806 and 1807 the Quarter-Eagles coined bear upon the obverse head of Liberty, above the word "Liberty," and below the date of the year of issue. Reverse: An eagle, from its beak a scroll with "E Pluribus Unum" upon it; around the head of the eagle are thirteen stars above a curved line of clouds, the whole surrounded by the words "United States of America."

In 1808 a slight alteration was made in the coinage of Quarter-Eagles. They bear upon the obverse the head of

Liberty, with the word "Liberty" in a curved line above the head, and below the head the date 1808. Upon the reverse they have an eagle, wings uplifted, from its beak a scroll, upon which is inscribed "E Pluribus Unum;" above the head thirteen stars and a curved line of clouds, the whole surrounded by an almost circle with the words, "United States of America."

From 1809, and up to 1820, inclusive, no Quarter-Eagles were coined.

In 1821 an entire new device was adopted for the Quarter-Eagles. They bear upon the obverse head of Liberty, facing to the left, wearing a kind of turban, a band encircling the same, upon which the word "Liberty;" above the head thirteen stars, below "1821." Reverse: An eagle with U. S. shield upon its breast, an olive branch and three arrows in its talons, above a scroll inscribed, "E Pluribus Unum;" around the whole the words, "United States of America," and below "2½ D."

During 1822 and 1823 none were issued.

During 1824, 1825, 1826 and 1827 the same devices and inscriptions as those upon the Quarter-Eagles of 1821 were continued, with the exception of the change of date of each respective year's coinage.

During 1828 no Quarter-Eagles were issued.

During 1829, 1830, 1831, 1832 and 1833, the same devices and inscriptions as those upon the Quarter-Eagles of 1821 were continued, with the substitution of the date of the year of issue.

During 1834, there were two distinct coinages of Quarter-Eagles. The first coinage was similar in every particular with the exception of the date "1834" as those of 1821. The second coinage bears upon the obverse: Head of Liberty, facing to the left, hair confined by a band upon which is inscribed: "Liberty;" the whole surrounded by thirteen stars, and below the date "1834." Reverse: Eagle with uplifted wings, U. S. shield upon its breast, in its talons an olive branch and arrows; the whole surrounded by thirteen stars, below "2½ D."

During 1835, 1836, 1837, 1838 and 1839, inclusive, the same devices and inscriptions as those upon the Quarter-Eagles of 1834 were continued, with the exception of the change of date of each respective year's coinage.

In 1840 a new device was once more adopted for the Quarter-Eagle. They bear upon the obverse: Liberty, head facing to the left, hair tied behind, a coronet upon the forehead, on which is inscribed: "Liberty;" the whole surrounded by thirteen stars: below the date "1839." Reverse: Eagle with the U. S. shield upon its breast, olive branch and three arrows in the talons. The whole is surrounded by thirteen stars, and below "2½ D."

Since 1840 and up to the present time the same devices and inscriptions were continued, with the exception of the change of date of each respective year's coinage.

THREE DOLLARS.—The Three Dollar Gold piece was authorized to be coined by Act of February 2, 1853, its weight fixed at 77.4 grains, and of 900 fineness.

In 1854 the first coinage of the Three Dollar gold pieces took place. They bear upon the obverse: A female head, designed to represent an Indian princess, the head with flowing hair is encircled by feathers in a band around the same, on which is inscribed the word: Liberty." The whole is surrounded by the words: "United States of America. Upon the Reverse: "3 Dollars 1854," occupying the field and inscribed in three lines; the whole surrounded by a wreath consisting of corn, wheat cotton and tobacco.

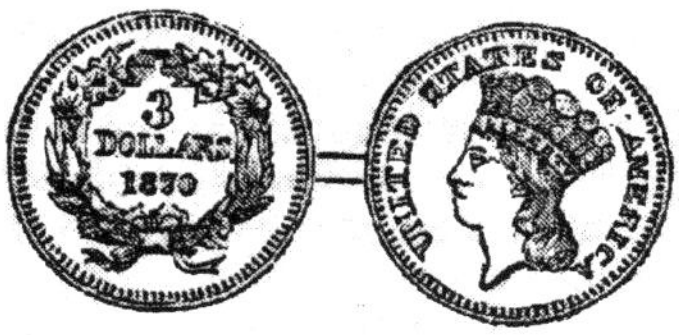
3
DOLLARS
1870
UNITED STATES OF AMERICA

No change has been made since in the coinage of the Three Dollar gold pieces, the same devices and inscriptions have been continued, with the exception of the change of date of each respective year's issue.

ONE DOLLAR.—The Gold Dollar was first authorized to be coined by Act of March 3, 1849, its weight fixed at 25.8 grains, and its fineness at 900.

In 1849, the first Gold Dollars were coined. They bear upon the obverse: A head of Liberty facing to the left, and wearing a coronet, the hair tied behind and curls falling over the neck. The whole is surrounded by thirteen stars. Reverse: "1 Dollar 1849," occupying the field and inscribed in three lines within a laurel wreath, The whole is surrounded by the words: "United States of America."

In 1850, 1851, 1852, 1853, inclusive, the same devices and inscriptions as upon the Gold Dollar of 1849 were continued, with the exception of the change of date of each respective year's coinage.

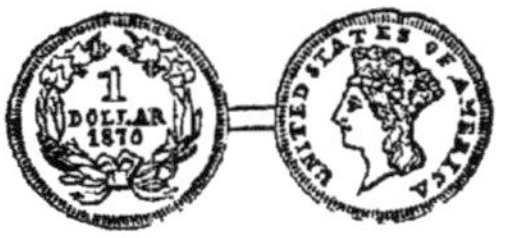
1
DOLLAR
1870
UNITED STATES OF AMERICA

In 1854 there were two distinct coinages of Gold Dollars; the first was similar in every particular to the previous year's coinages, while the second was changed even in size, the same being slightly increased; but the weight and fineness remained the same. This second coinage bears upon the Obverse: A female head, designed to represent an Indian princess; the head with flowing hair is encircled by feathers in a band around the same, upon which is inscribed the word: "Liberty." The whole is surrounded by the words: "United States of America." Upon the Reverse: "1 Dollar 1854," occupying the field and inscribed in three lines; the whole surrounded by a wreath consisting of corn, wheat cotton and tobacco.

No change has been made since in the coinage of the Gold Dollar, the same devices and inscriptions have been continued, with the exception of the change of date of each respective year's issue.

Silver Coins.

One Dollar—The first U. S. Dollar was issued from the Mint in the latter part of the year 1794. The number of pieces was small; they are consequently highly valued, especially when in fine condition. A very high price was paid for a perfect specimen at the sale of M. L. Mackenzie in 1869. The bust on this and all others of the old Dollars looks toward the observer's right. The hair is flowing, date beneath and "Liberty" above the bust which is naked. There are seven stars facing and eight behind; on the reverse an eagle stands upon a support, with raised wings; he is surrounded with two half wreaths joined below by a ribbon; legend, "United States of America;" the edge is lettered "Hundred Cents One Dollar or unit," the words being separated by stars and sunken square marks.

The Dollars of 1795 are many of them precisely like those of 1794, with the change of date, but towards the latter part of the year a great change was made. The hair is quite curly and the ends of a fillet are seen tied behind. The bust is draped and only six stars are found facing and seven behind; on the reverse side the eagle rests upon a cloud.

No change in the Dollar, except slight variations in the several dies, until 1798. This year we find both fifteen and

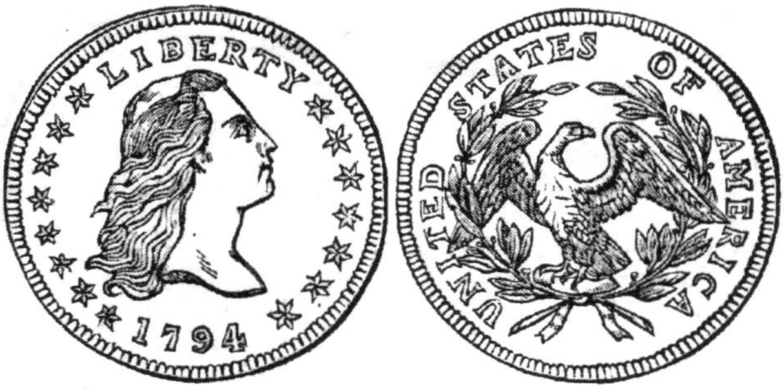
LIBERTY
1794
UNITED STATES OF AMERICA

thirteen stars, with the eagle above described, called the small eagle, on the reverse. But they are scarce and both bring a good premium. The larger emission of the year—and it was very plentiful—has what is called the large eagle. The bird is displayed; a bundle of arrows is clasped in the right talon, an olive branch in the left; the breast is covered with a shield, argent, six pales gules, a chief azure; the

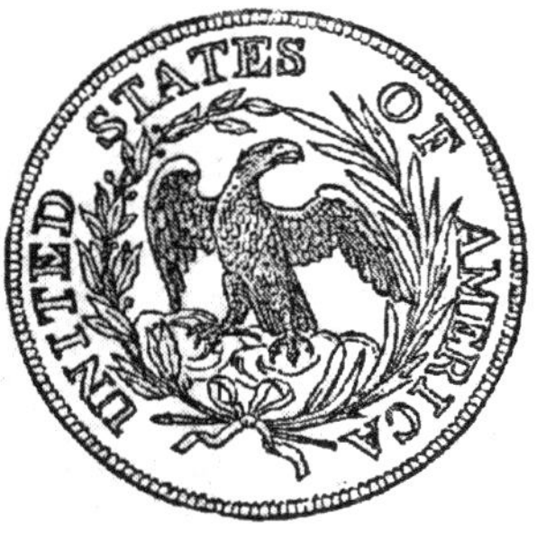
UNITED STATES OF AMERICA

beak holds a scroll inscribed "E Pluribus Unum;" above the head are thirteen stars, with an arched canopy of eight clouds; the legend, "United States of America," is in large letters.

In 1799 one variety has five instead of six stars facing, otherwise the Dollars after 1798 are like the larger emission of that year, with unimportant exceptions, until 1804. Those of the latter year are very rare, probably not over ten genuine original pieces being known. It is alleged the dies were not made in 1804, but many years later, to be used in

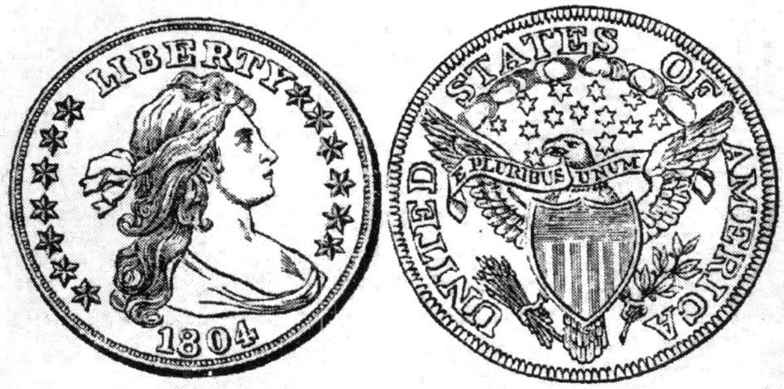
LIBERTY
1804
STATES OF AMERICA
UNITED
PLURIBUS UNUM

presenting the pieces to a foreign representative. They have sold at auction at prices varying from $350 to $750, Col. Cohen's bringing the first-named sum and J. J. Mickley's the last.

From 1804 to 1835, inclusive, we do not find any U. S. Dollars. In 1836 a beautifully designed piece, the work of Christian Gobrecht, appeared. The Goddess of Liberty for the first time appears seated. She is looking backwards, towards the observer's left, her left hand grasps a liberty pole surmounted by a cap, the right rests on a shield similar to that already described on the Dollar of 1798, only more ornate. A scroll with the word "Liberty" issues from the hand and rests upon the shield; date below. "C. Gobrecht F" on the base of the support. Reverse, an eagle volant; above and beneath him, twenty-six stars, typifying that number of States, although the Union then contained but twenty-five. Legend, "United States of America, One Dollar." One thousand Dollars of 1836, it is claimed, were struck in that year of the above-described pattern. In addition to these, eighteen others, differing in having the name of Gobrecht in the field above the date instead of upon the support, were also coined. Being rare, a Dollar of the last-named variety has brought a very high price. Of the other, a fine proof can be had for from twelve to fifteen dollars.

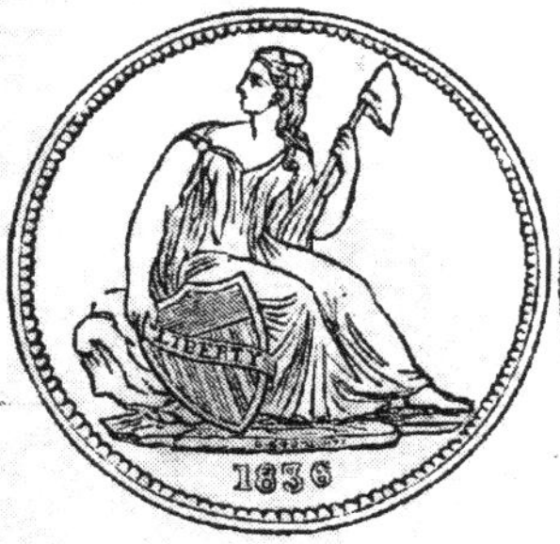
LIBERTY
1836
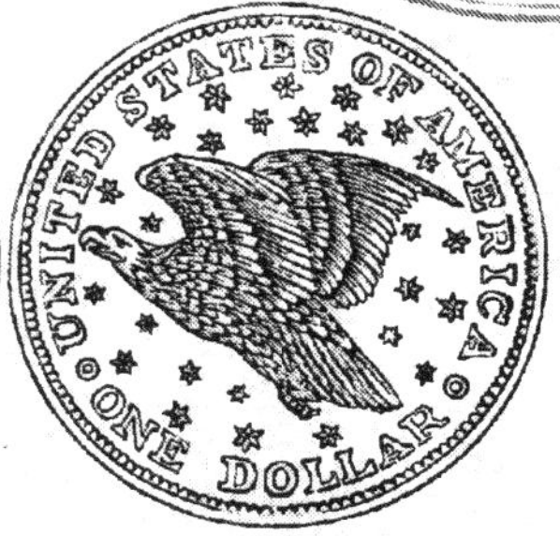
UNITED STATES OF AMERICA
ONE DOLLAR

No Dollars were issued from the Mint in the year 1837. In 1838 a limited number was coined, the design differing from those in 1836, on the obverse, in having thirteen stars around the figure of Liberty seated, seven of the number being toward her right hand, five toward her left and one between the head and cap. On the reverse the stars are omitted, leaving the field between the eagle and the legend plain. A fine proof Dollar of 1838 sells for about forty dollars.

In 1839 the same designs were adopted. The issue was larger than the year previous, but still sufficiently small to make them bring twenty-five to thirty dollars in 1882.

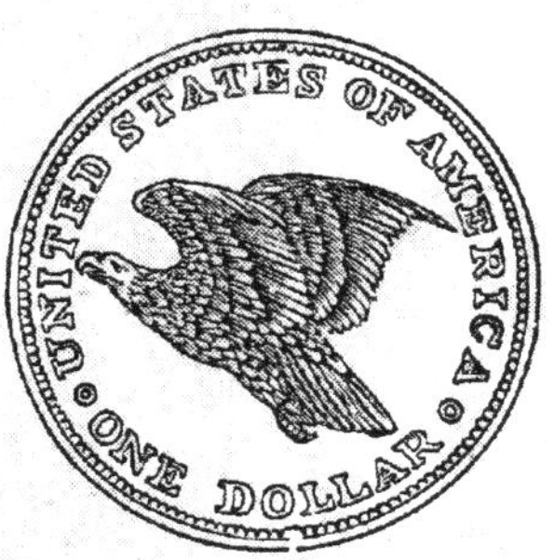
UNITED STATES OF AMERICA
ONE DOLLAR

The obverse design of 1838 was continued on the American Dollar until 1873, when the Trade Dollar was adopted. The reverse, however, was changed in 1840. The eagle here is displayed; a shield similar to that on the old Dollar reverse, only smaller, is shown upon his breast. The left talon has three arrows in it, the right has the olive branch. Below these, "One Dol." This style of reverse was continued into 1865. In 1866 there was an addition made of a scroll above the eagle, inscribed "In God we Trust." No other change was made until 1873.

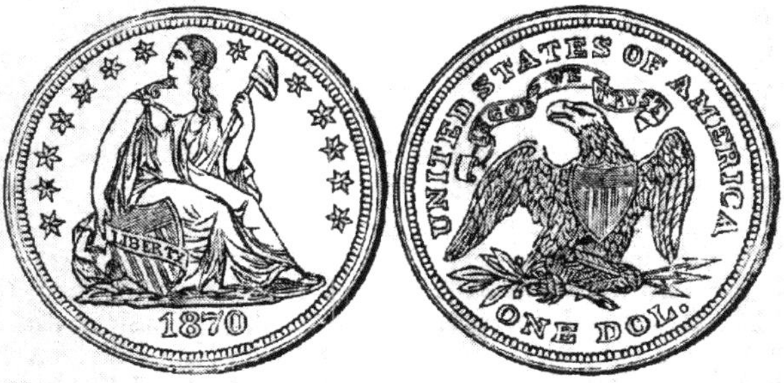
LIBERTY
1870
UNITED STATES OF AMERICA
ONE DOL.

Before the adoption of the Trade Dollar, seven patterns were made and submitted to Congress to select from. The ugliest of them all, as regards the obverse, was chosen. A giantess eight feet high, representing the Goddess of Liberty, looking towards the left hand, is seated on a bale of cotton. A sheaf of wheat seems to assist the cotton in giving her support. Her left hand grasps a dimly defined scroll, inscribed "Liberty," trailing over the bale. The right hand seems to be shaking an olive branch at some unseen object. On the base is inscribed "In God we Trust." Four stars face the lady, two are between her head and the branch and

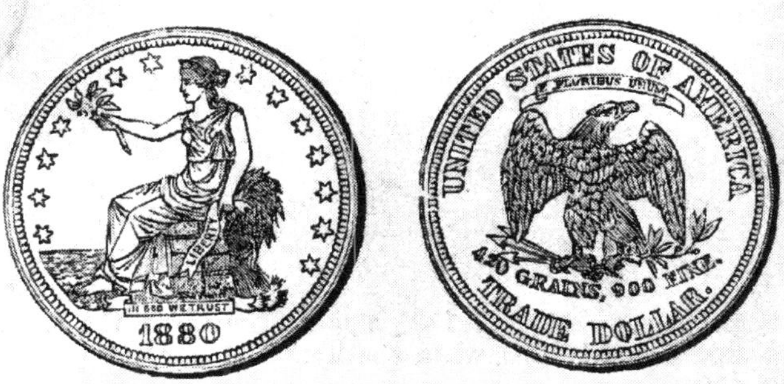
1880
UNITED STATES OF AMERICA
TRADE DOLLAR.

seven are behind her. Reverse; an eagle displayed, rampant. The right talon has three arrows, the left a nondescript branch that it might puzzle botanists to explain. A scroll above the eagle's head is inscribed "E Pluribus Unum." Legend: "United States of America, Trade Dollar, 420 grains, 900 fine." Trade Dollars were coined from 1873 to 1882. A bill for their abolition is under consideration.

In 1878 the Standard or Bland Dollar was adopted. Here we have a classic head, said to be taken from a young lady in Philadelphia. The hair is banged, curled, tied with a band inscribed "Liberty," has a wreath of cereals around it and a small cap. Seven stars are facing and six behind; above, "E Pluribus Unum" in large Roman letters

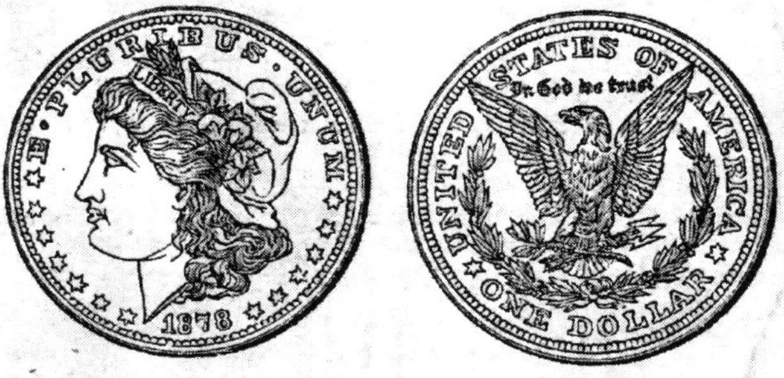
E PLURIBUS UNUM
LIBERTY
1878
UNITED STATES OF AMERICA
In God we trust
ONE DOLLAR

and the date below. Reverse, similar in design to the last, but differing greatly in execution. The eagle has enormous wings, the arrows and branch are reversed. "In God we Trust," in a straight line and in Gothic characters apppears above. "United States of America" and "One Dollar" are separated by two stars. There are also two consecutive half wreaths, beneath and around the eagle, fastened below with a ribbon. On the ordinary Dollar, the eagle has seven feathers in the tail. Originally the bird had eight feathers; In 1878 the die was changed and one feather omitted unintentionally by the engraver. Of the eight feathered variety, it is said but fifty specimens were made, in proof condition, and not a few were made for general circulation, consequently they are not rare.

HALF DOLLARS.—The coinage of Half Dollars commenced the same year as that of the Dollars, that is in 1794. And the devices are the exact counterpart of each other, the only difference being simply in the proportional size of the two coins, and that the half is lettered on the edge "Fifty Cents or Half Dollar." The next year no change. In 1796 the counterpart of the Fillet Dollar of 1795 was adopted; the reverse is changed to a smaller eagle, standing on a cloud,

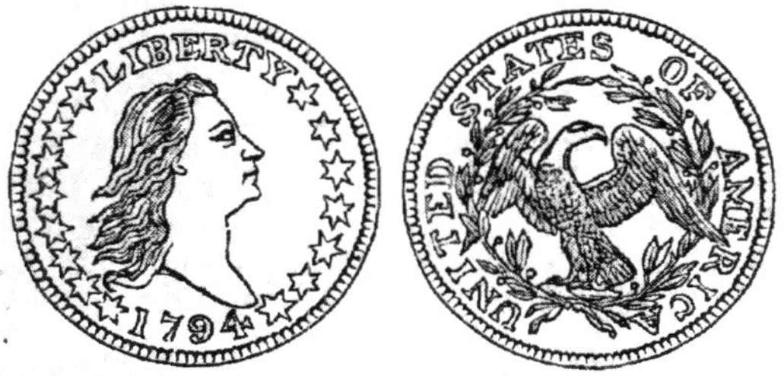
LIBERTY
1794
UNITED STATES OF AMERICA

with the fraction ½ underneath. This was also adopted in 1797; none were coined in 1798, 1799, 1800, 1804. In that of 1801, and ever after, the fraction was omitted, the reverse

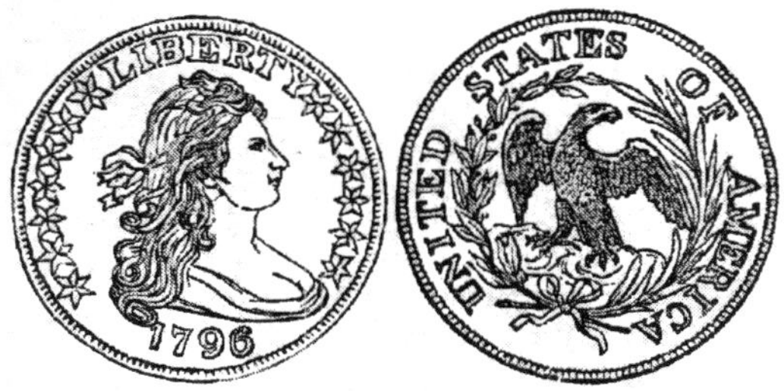
LIBERTY
1796
UNITED STATES OF AMERICA

being similar to that of the Dollar of the same year.

In 1807 the style of head of the Cent of 1808, with the addition of a cap, was adopted in the course of the year.

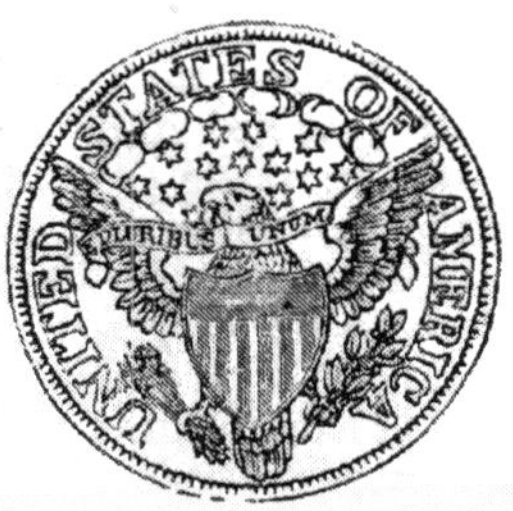
UNITED STATES OF AMERICA

Both this and the old style are found in circulation. On the reverse the device is similar to that of the Dollar of 1840

and afterwards, with the substitution of "50 C." instead of "One Dol.," and a scroll above inscribed "E Pluribus Unum." With the exception of 1816, when there was no

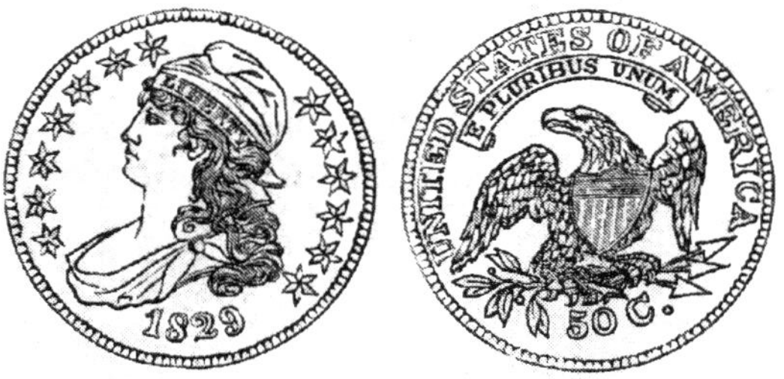
LIBERTY
1829
UNITED STATES OF AMERICA
E PLURIBUS UNUM
50 C.

silver coinage, this variety, with slight variations, was coined every year until 1836. In 1836, a smaller head was adopted the latter part of the year. This is known as the *Gobrecht*

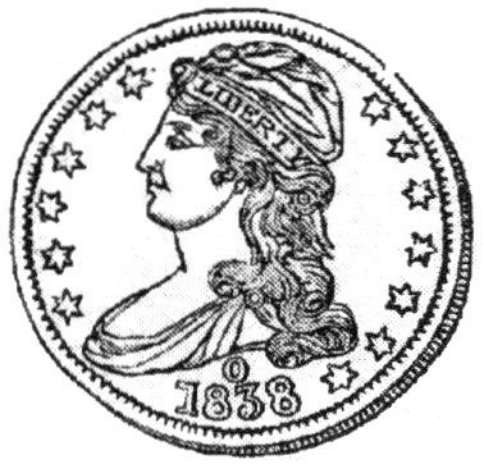
LIBERTY
O
1838

head, from the artist who designed it. The reverse has smaller letters, the scroll is omitted, "50 Cents" takes the place of "50 C.," and the edge is reeded instead of lettered. In 1838 "50 Cents" at the base is replaced by "Half Dol." In 1839 the obverse is changed to the Goddess of Liberty seated, both styles being made, and the small letters of the reverse being continued. In 1842 larger letters were again placed on the reverse. In 1853 there is a variety without rays or arrows, but very rare; the standard of the Half Dollar and other subsidiary coins was reduced in weight, and, in order to indicate the difference, arrows were placed on either side of the date, and on the reverse, rays were placed in the field around the eagle.

In 1854 the arrows were retained but the rays were omitted. No change in the obverse until 1873, when, owing to a change of standard, the arrows again appear, for that year and 1874 only. On the reverse in 1866 there is added, above the head of the eagle, a scroll inscribed "In God we trust." This is continued until the present time.

1879
UNITED STATES OF AMERICA
HALF DOL.

Of the Half Dollars there are several that have excited the interest of collectors, on account of being overstrikes of previous years. For instance, 1808 over 1807, 1817 over 1813, 1818 over 1817, etc.

UNITED STATES OF AMERICA

UNITED STATES OF AMERICA
25 C.

LIBERTY
1796

QUARTER DOLLARS.—The first Quarter came from the Mint in 1796. The devices are those of the Dollar in every part exactly; but the edge is reeded and not lettered. This is true of all U. S. Quarter Dollars. Although this Quarter is quite scarce, bringing in perfect condition twenty-five dollars, the supply seems to have sufficed until the year 1804, when the coinage was renewed, and a limited number appeared. They are nearly as scarce as those of 1796, and sell for little less. The reverse of this, as well as that of 1805-6 and 7, has the displayed eagle with clouds above, similar to the Dollars and Halves of the early part of this century. The latter dates are common in circulation, but in fine condition they bring several dollars, the 1807 being considered most desirable.

Again there was a recess in the coinage, and not until the year 1815 did they again appear, similar in obverse and reverse to the Half Dollar of 1815. None were coined in 1816

1815
UNITED STATES OF AMERICA
E PLURIBUS UNUM
25 C.

or 1817; in 1818 they were made in abundance, being similar to that of 1815. This style continued to be made in 1819 –20, 21, 22, 23, 24, 25, 27 and 28. Again an interval. In 1831 the head is smaller, the label is omitted, and the letters, etc., are smaller. There was a change also in 1838: two types—Bust, and Liberty seated. Every year thereafter, up to the present time, there has been no intermission. In 1823 the coinage was very limited. A Quarter Dollar of this year has been known to sell for about a hundred dollars, and very poor pieces bring twenty or thirty dollars.

UNITED STATES OF AMERICA
25 C.

In 1827 only four pieces, as alleged by the late Joseph J. Mickley, were made, all of which he obtained at face value in that year. But of latter time the old dies have been found, and a number of pieces were made from them. They are readily known, as the dies were rusty and had to be cleaned, and the impression shows that this was done.

In 1838 the change to Liberty seated was made, similar to the Dollar adopted in 1840; of course "Quar. Dol." takes the place of "One Dol." on the reverse. Both styles are found. In 1853 we have the arrows by the date and the rays around the eagle, as in the halves of the same year, and a few are found without them. In 1854-5 the arrows, but not rays. In 1866 the scroll inscribed "In God we trust" was adopted, and is still in use. In 1873-4 the arrows again. Excepting those mentioned as desirable, all the Quarters can be obtained without much search, the scarcer of the common ones being considered 1815 and 1866.

1879
UNITED STATES OF AMERICA
QUAR. DOL.

Overstrikes will be found in 1806 over '05, 1823 over '22 1824 over '23 and 1825 over '24.

Twenty Cent Pieces.—These are similar on the obverse, to the quarter dollar of the corresponding years, they were coined; that is, from 1875 to 1878, inclusive. The reverse differs merely in the eagle, who looks toward the right; there is no motto or scroll, and "Twenty Cents" replaces "Quar.

1875
UNITED STATES OF AMERICA
TWENTY CENTS

Dollar." The edge is plain. Those dated 1875 and 1876 are common. Those of 1877 and 1878 are rare, being struck only in proof condition, bringing several dollars apiece, those of 1877 being considered most valuable.

LIBERTY
1796
UNITED STATES OF AMERICA
UNITED STATES OF AMERICA

Dimes.—The issue of dimes was first made in the year 1796. They are the exact counterpart in every way of the quarter dollar of the same year, having the same devices, the

same number of stars and the small eagle resting on the clouds, but of proportionately small size and weight, to make it the tenth instead of the fourth part of a dollar. In 1797 there was no change excepting in the date, and in one variety which has sixteen stars. In 1798, the reverse has the large eagle under the clouds, like the quarter of 1804. Dimes were

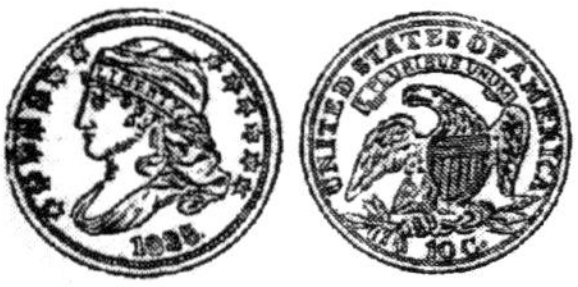

coined in 1800, 1, 2, 3, 4, 5 and 7, precisely like those of 1798. In 1809 they were changed to correspond with the quarters of 1815, "10c." being substituted for "25c." This style continued until the year 1836, inclusive, omitting the years 1810, 12, 13, 15, 16, 17, 18, 19 and 26. In 1828 there were large and small dates.

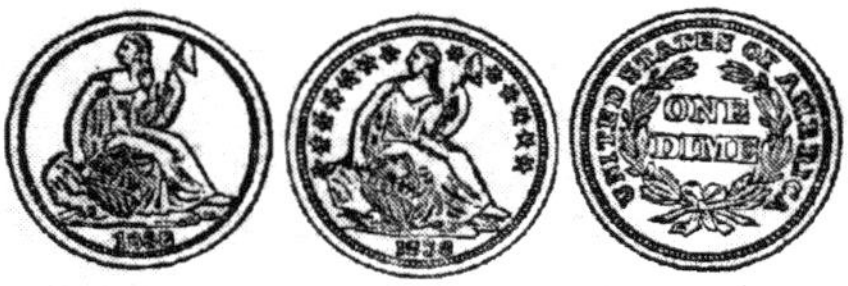
ONE
DIME

There were overstrikes in 1798, 1811, 1814 and 1824. In 1837 Liberty seated appears, with the stars omitted on the obverse, and on the reverse "One Dime" in two lines, surrounded by a wreath having "United States of America," encircling it around the border. In 1838 the stars are added similar to the quarters of the same date. The dimes from 1839 to 1859, inclusive, are like those of 1838, excepting that in one variety of 1853, and all those of 1854 and 5, there are arrows on each side of the date. In 1860 another change is

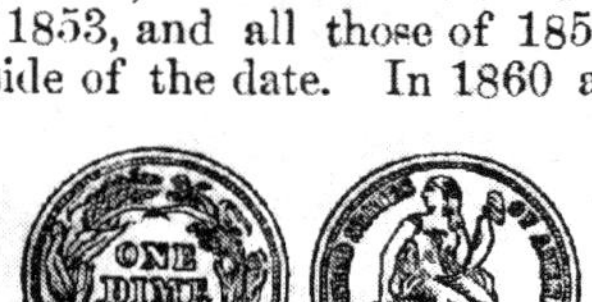
ONE
DIME

seen in the omission of the stars and substitution of "United States of America," on the obverse; and on the reverse a wreath

of cereals surrounds the words "One Dime" in two lines, which occupies the centre. No variation in the dime has since been made up to the present time, excepting that part of the issue of 1873 and all that of 1874 has arrows on each side of the date.

The following dimes are most valuable to the collector: 1804, 1800, 22, 1, 2 3 1797, 98, 1809, 1796, 1811, 5, 7, 46.

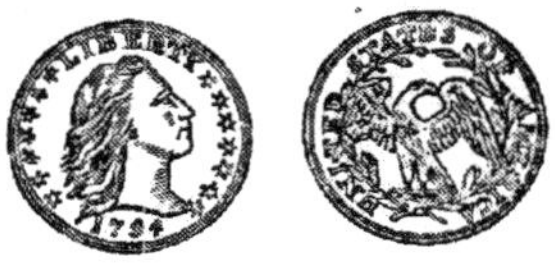

HALF DIMES.—These were first coined in the year 1794, and in this and the next year they are the exact counterpart of the half dollar of the same year, only reduced in size and weight corresponding to their denomination, and they had fourteen instead of thirteen stars. In 1796 the dimes of the

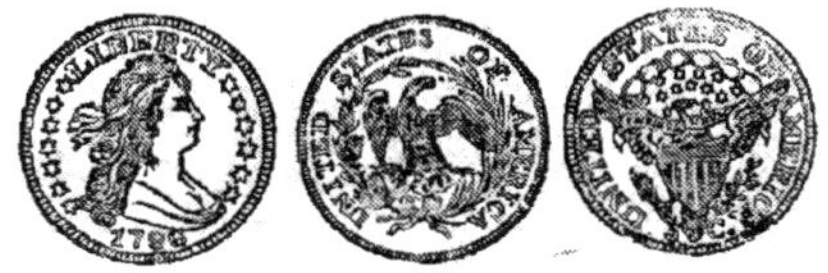

same year where copied, with fifteen stars. The same style occurs in 1797, in which year there are three varieties, with thirteen, fifteen, and sixteen stars. From 1800 to 1805, inclusive, they have thirteen stars on the obverse, while the large eagle reverse is adopted.

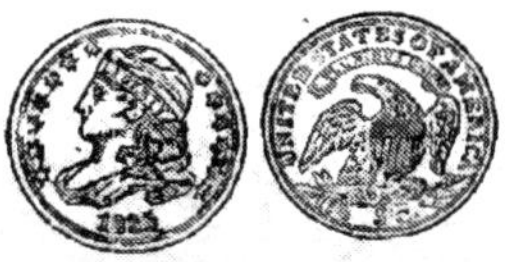

After 1805 no half dimes appeared until after the year 1829 when they were reproduced and continued to be issued each year without interruption until in 1873 the coin was discontinued. From 1829 to 1837 inclusive, the style of the half dollars of corresponding years was adopted for the half dimes. The latter year, Liberty seated, without stars, like the dime of 1837, was emitted plentifully. In 1838, Liberty seated, with stars, was adopted, and continued to be used up to the year 1860. The changes noted in the dime of this latter year were made at the same time in the half dime.

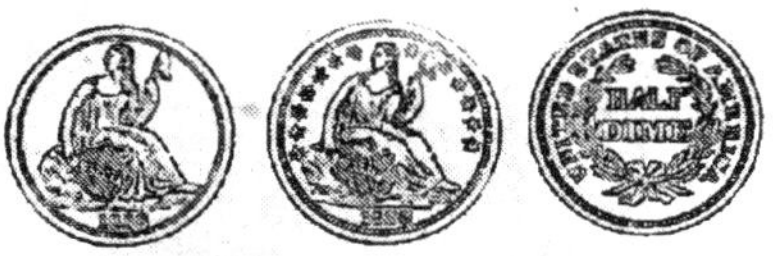
HALF
DIME

Three Cent Pieces.—These first appeared in 1851, and were discontinued in 1873. For three years they were alloyed with 25 per cent of copper. In and after 1854 their

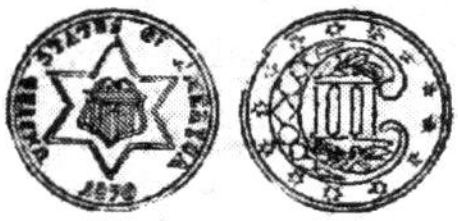

fineness was raised to that of the silver of larger denominations. The device is a letter "C" enclosing three numerals, and surrounded by thirteen stars. Reverse: A star bearing a shield. Legend: "United States of America." The date is below. In 1854 the large star has sharper points, and there is an addition on the reverse of an olive branch above and a bundle of arrows below the numerals. No other change was made after this date.

The dates sought after are 1855 and all after, and including 1863.

Nickel Coins.

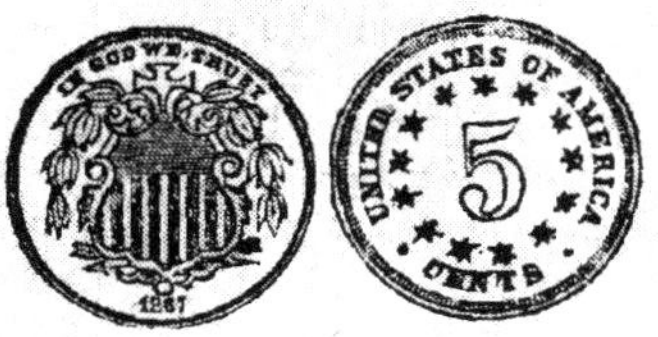
IN GOD WE TRUST
1867
UNITED STATES OF AMERICA
5
CENTS

These consist of alloy 25 per cent. nickel to 75 copper. The larger coin first appeared in 1866. A figure "5" is surrounded with a circle of thirteen stars, separated by rays pointing inwards. Legend: "United States of America."

below is the word "Cents." Reverse; a shield decorated, the base resting on crossed arrows. Above is the legend, "In God we Trust." In 1867 the rays were omitted from the obverse; no other change has since occurred.

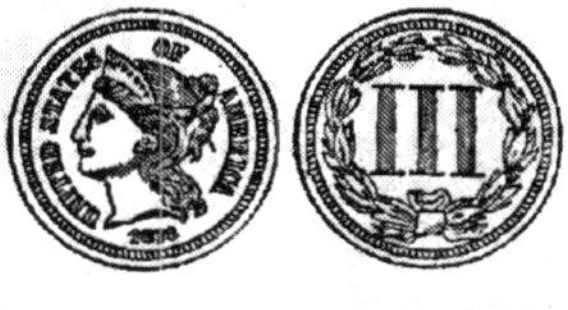
III

On the Three Cent coins a head of Liberty, looking right, is surrounded by the legend "United States of America," and the date is below. Reverse: Three numerals surrounded by a wreath. It has been coined every year since the first issue in 1865.

Copper Coins.

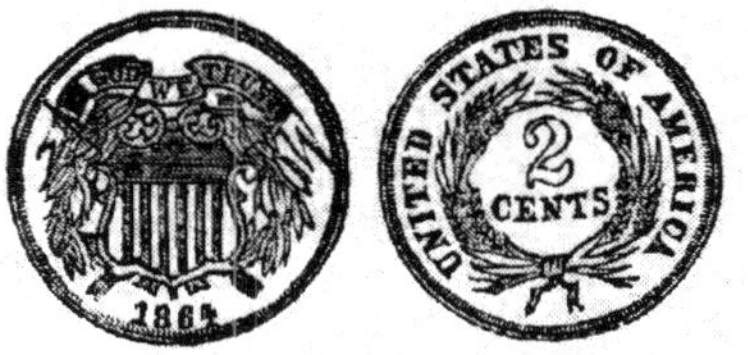
1864
UNITED STATES OF AMERICA
2
CENTS

Two Cents.—This coin first appeared in 1864, and was discontinued in 1873. The alloy was the same as the cent of the same period, and its weight 96 grains. "2 Cents," in two lines, is enclosed by two half wreaths of wheat, tied at the lower ends. Legend: "United States of America;" reverse similar in design to the nickel Five Cent pieces, only the legend is in a scroll, and the crossed arrows, upon which the shield rests, seems to support its centre instead of its base. The Two Cent piece of 1872 is scarce; that of 1873, being only in proof sets, is very scarce.

One Cent.—There are four pattern cents bearing the date 1792, whether made in or designed to be used by the U. S. Mint is uncertain. They are all extremely rare. The largest, which exceeds the Half-Dollar in size, has on the obverse a head of Liberty with flowing hair, which partly covers the bust on both sides, and faces toward the observer's right; the date in large figures, is immediately beneath the bust, and the legend is "Liberty Parent of Science and Industry." On the shoulder of the bust is the name of Birch; on the reverse, in the centre, are the words "One Cent," surrounded by a circle; this is surrounded by a wreath, and it again by the legend "United States of America."

The second in size is a trifle less in diameter than the Half-Dollar. Obverse: A naked bust of Liberty, facing right, with the hair confined by a band and knot, beneath it "1792," above it "Liberty." Reverse: An eagle, his wings raised, standing on a section of a globe, facing right; legend, "United States of America." Only two of these are now known, one of them being in the Mint Cabinet.

The small pattern cents are about the diameter of the present Quarter-Dollar, the only difference between them is that one of them has a plug of silver in the centre. They are both from the same dies. Obverse: Head of Liberty with flowing hair, looking toward the right; date, 1792 under the bust. Legend: "Liberty Parent of Science and Industry;" reverse, "One Cent" in a wreath, and legend "United States of America;" at the base, $\frac{1}{100}$.

But it was not until the succeeding year, 1793, that the operations of the Mint were productive of much relief to the community in the matter of a circulating medium. Only the copper pieces were made this year. Of the cent there were three distinct styles and several varieties of dies of both obverse and reverse.

1. *Chain Cents.*—These have a bust with flowing hair, looking right, with the date below and word "Liberty" above it; on the reverse side, in the centre, is "One Cent," with "$\frac{1}{100}$" below it enclosed in an endless chain of fifteen

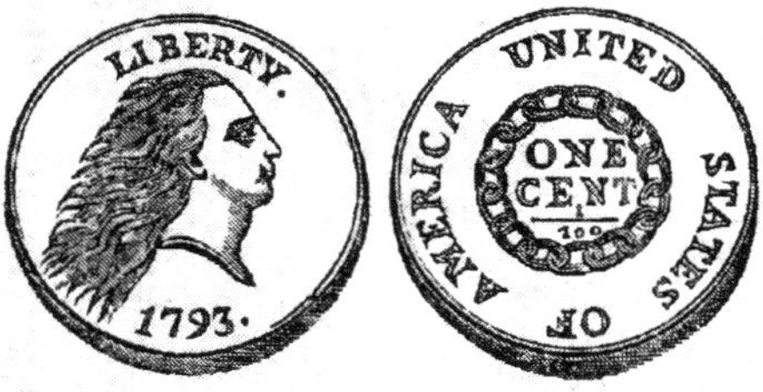
LIBERTY.
1793.
UNITED STATES OF AMERICA
ONE
CENT
1/100

links, typifying the number of States then in the Union. The legend is "United States of America" in all excepting one die, which reads "United States of Ameri," the engraver evidently not having room to complete the word. This being quite scarce is highly prized by some collectors of cents. The edges have in four sections alternately a vine and several bars.

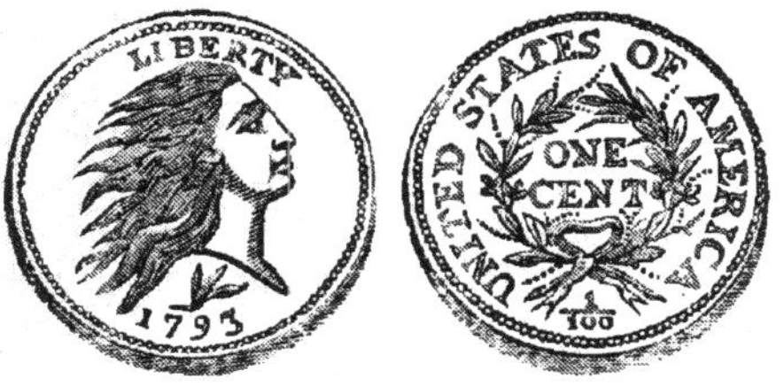
LIBERTY
1793
UNITED STATES OF AMERICA
ONE CENT
1/100

2. *Wreath Cents.*—Obverse, a bust with disheveled hair flowing freely, beneath it a sprig, in most cases of three figs or olive leaves; in a very rare variety it is of shamrock. The reverse has two half wreaths, fastened by a ribbon at the bottom, the $\frac{1}{100}$ below and legend at the last; both sides have a beaded circle around the edge. Many wreath Cents have the vine and bars; but one variety has the words "One Hundred for a Dollar" on the edge.

3. *Liberty Cap Cent.*—These are larger in diameter, and are all lettered on the edge "One Hundred for a Dollar." The letters on the obverse and reverse are larger than either of the preceding, and the beaded circles on the edges are more bold and striking than in the last. On the obverse the flowing hair bust has a Liberty cap on a pole extending across and behind it.

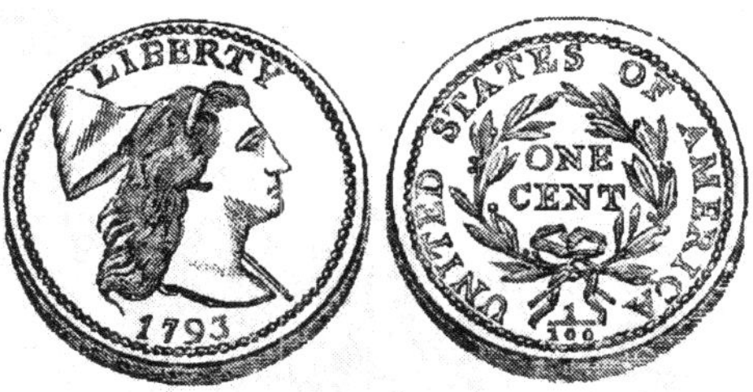
LIBERTY
1793
UNITED STATES OF AMERICA
ONE CENT
1/100

In its general character, the Cent of 1794 resembles the Liberty Cap Cent of 1793. It is slightly thicker and proportionately smaller in diameter. Instead of the beaded border, it has a serrated milling on both sides. Many dies were used during the year, whose slight variations have afforded a study to coin collectors. One of them resembles its prede-cessor in date almost exactly. Two others differ only in a slight degree. In others the letters and figures vary in size, position, etc., as also do the bust, cap, pole, different parts of the half wreaths and their connecting ribbon. Some of them approach in style the Cent of 1795 and one is its exact coun-terpart. The essential difference between the main issues of 1794 and 1795 being that in the latter year the two or more adjoining hairs appear to be plaited together just be-fore the termination. These varieties are hence sometimes called the " Plicæ." The lower combination, or plait, also makes less of a hook at the end in the 1795's.

On the reverse the most notable differences are, in one the absence of a dividing line in the fraction, and in another a ring of eighty-nine minute stars arranged around the periph-ery, some of them more or less obliterated by the milling. Both of these varieties are quite rare. We have seen three only of each.

Of the Cent and Half-Cent of 1795 we have the lettered and the unlettered edge variety. The latter are lightest in weight, in accordance with a law changing the standard for the future. In a few cabinets is found a cent, bearing date of 1795, that is wholly different in artistic make from all other Cents ; the hair is much finer and brushed out nearly straight : the lowest lock however, is shaped like the letter S laid on its side ; the profile and high check bones suggest those of an Indian. Some people imagine a resem-blance to the portrait of Thomas Jefferson ; hence it is pop-ularly known as the " Jefferson Head Cent." The execution of the reverse is equally distinguishing ; the ribbon bow has three instead of two turns: the leaves are longer, the berries smaller and more numerous and the stems finer than in any other United States Cent. Its origin is a mystery, some be-lieve it to have been a pattern, while others with more prob-ability assign it to a counterfeiter. At all events it is suffi-ciently rare now to bring a good price ; one hundred and forty-five dollars has been paid for the best specimen known to the large body of collectors.

The Cents of this year, with lettered edges, are rarer than those without the lettering. They made a Liberty Cap Cent in 1796. There was also made a new style of obverse during this year, which also was used in 1797 and 1798. For the first time the bust is draped. A fillet on the back of head is revealed by its bow; but the hairs general-ly end in curls, one on the cheek, two on the neck and several others behind. The liberty cap is omitted, as is the lettering on the edge, never to reappear on the American Cent.

Both varieties of the Cent of 1796 are not rare, one about as plentiful as the other. But in an uncirculated condition, the Liberty Cap is much less seldom seen than the other and will command about double the price.

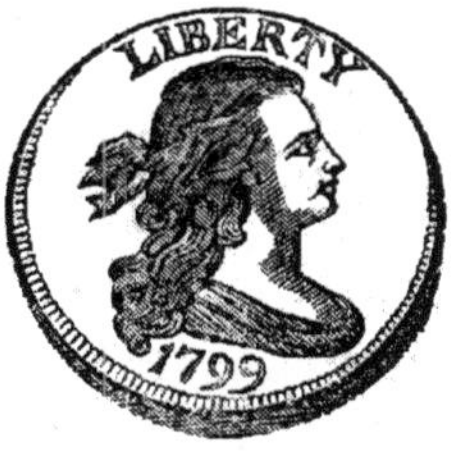
LIBERTY
1799

In 1797 no change to remark.

In the year 1798 a slight change was made in the obverse of the Cent, giving some of the curls a different termination from those of 1796, '97, and the early part of 1798. The latter device was continued each year, until and including 1807. The reverse remained unchanged until the same time, excepting some slight variations, probably unintentional, if not positive mistakes. For instance, in 1797 and 1802 we find some without stems to the wreaths, and in one case only one stem. In 1801 and 1802 some have $\frac{1}{000}$ instead of the fraction $\frac{1}{100}$. In addition to this error, a variety of the Cent of 1802 has "Iinited," instead of "United." In 1796 we have in one instance "Liherty," instead of "Liberty."

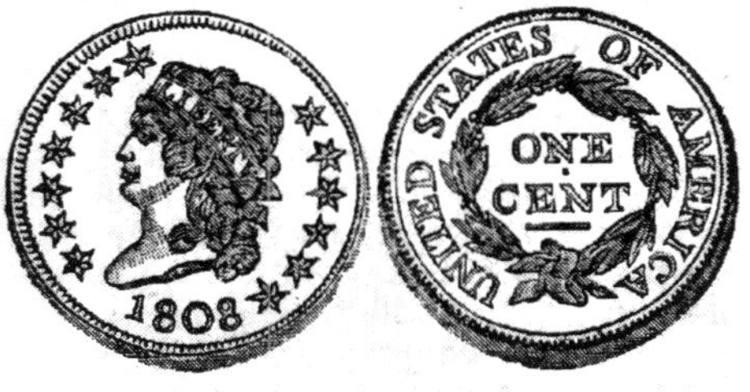
1808
UNITED STATES OF AMERICA
ONE CENT

In the changes made in 1808 an entirely new head was designed, facing left. Seven stars are to the left and six to the right. The head has a band tied across it, inscribed with the word "Liberty," and the hair is curled gracefully below the bands on the reverse. There is but one wreath, with the ends tied together, entirely encircling the words "One Cent," in two lines, with a point between them and the line below. This style continued until the year 1814, inclusive. It was also adopted on the Half Cent from 1809 to 1811, inclusive, when these coins were omitted until 1825. The same devices were then resumed until and including 1836, none being made in 1827 and 1830, and one variety in 1828 has but twelve stars.

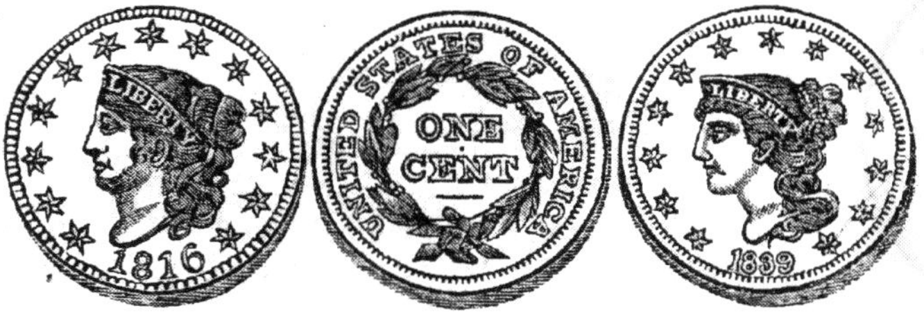
LIBERTY
1816
UNITED STATES OF AMERICA
ONE CENT
LIBERTY
1839

In 1815 no Cents were made at the United States Mint. In 1816 we have a different obverse. The head is broader than that of 1808, etc., and the hair is "put up" in a knot at the back part. The stars surround the bust at regular intervals. This style with some variations, was continued until the abolition of the old copper Cent in 1857, and the adoption of the nickel Cent in its place; the most noticeable changes being the following: In 1817 one variety has fifteen instead of thirteen stars. In 1838 the plain string that confines the hair is replaced by a beaded string, which was adopted thereafter. In 1839 there are five varieties, one of them is from an altered die of 1836.

A second has the head and reverse of 1838. A third has a lock on the forehead, and from the simple expression, is sometimes called the "Silly head." A fourth has also a remarkable expression, and is called the "Booby head." The line and point on the reverse are left off in this. The fifth variety has a smaller head, less curly and more old maidish in execution. The stars are smaller and the letters on the reverse are larger. This last was continued until 1857.

Overstrikes of Cents occurred in 1798 over 1797, 1799 over 1798, 1800, over 1799, 1807 over 6, 10 over 9, 11 over 10, 19 over 18, 20 over 19, 23 and 24 both over 22, and 39 over 36. In the Half-Cent series, we have 1802 over 1800, and 8 over 7.

The most valuable Cents are about in the following order: 1795 Jefferson head, 1799, 1804, 1793, 1809, 11, 6, 1796, 95, 1823. A fine Jefferson head has sold for $145. But fine cents of common dates often bring large prices. The sale of Mortimer McKenzie, in 1869, was the most successful, 88 Cents realizing $1295.

A really fine set of Cents is worth $300 to $500, a fine set of Half-Cents, about $200.

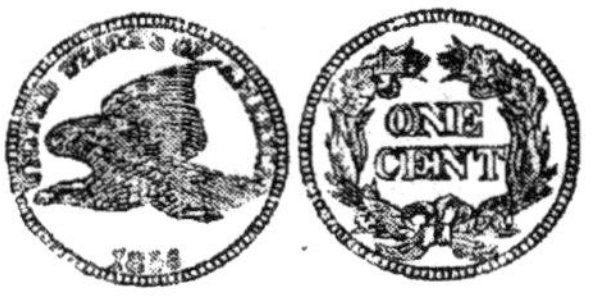
ONE
CENT

In 1856 the Cent was made of an alloy of copper 88 per cent. and nickel 12 per cent. The device was an eagle volant with the usual legend, "United States of America," and date below the device. Reverse, two half wreaths of cereals enclosing the words "One Cent." It weighed 72 grains. In 1859 the eagle was displaced by an Indian head, with a crown of feathers fastened by a band inscribed "Liberty" On the reverse the cereal wreath was displaced by a wreath

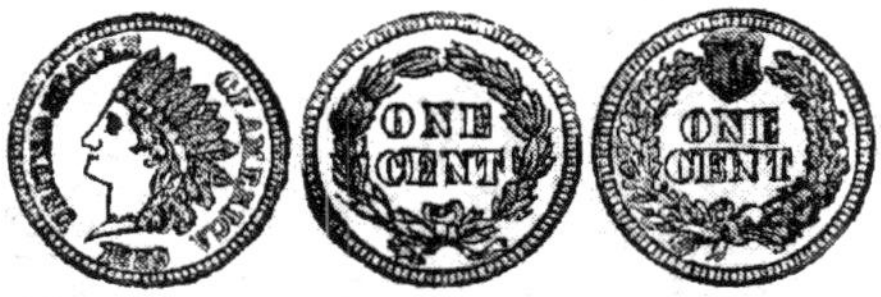
ONE
CENT
ONE
CENT

of laurel. In 1860 the reverse had a wreath of oak with a small shield separating the ends at the top. There has been no change in the designs of either side since 1860, but the alloy was changed in 1864 to copper 95 per cent. zinc and tin each 2½ per cent., and the weight to 48 grains.

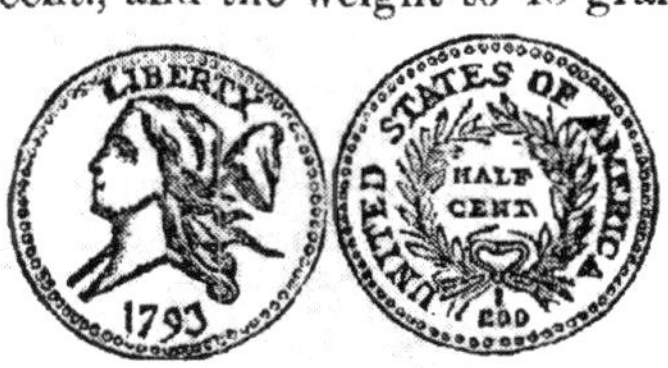
LIBERTY
1793
UNITED STATES OF AMERICA
HALF
CENT

Half Cent.—Of the Half-Cents of 1793 there were several dies, but only one variety. They have Liberty Caps like the

Cent but the bust faces towards the left, and the hair is confined by a fillet from the front and around the head; the edge is lettered "Two Hundred for a Dollar." The Half-Cent of 1794 is like the Cent of that year, Liberty Cap facing right, lettered edge same as 1793, there were several dies varying slightly the differences not of much interest, of

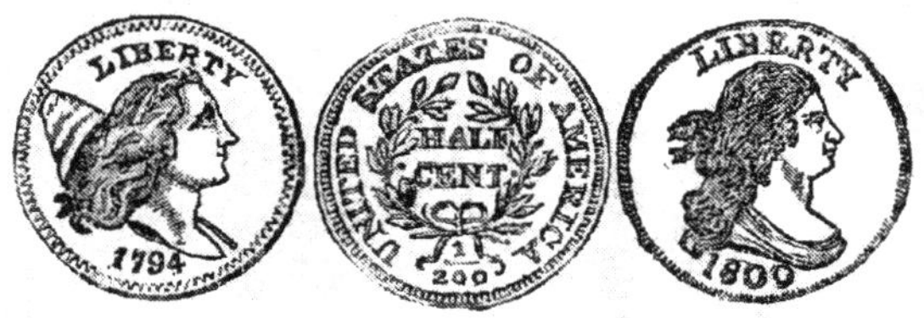
LIBERTY
1794
UNITED STATES OF AMERICA
HALF CENT
1
200
LIBERTY
1800

1795 are two varieties, lettered and unlettered edge, the latter is lightest in weight, in accordance with a law changing the standard weight for the future. Thick plancet lettered edge is the rarest of the two the 1796 Half-Cent is the rarest of all the Half Cents and a fine piece is worth over Twenty Dollars, 1797 is like the last, not very rare. We find one of this year with a lettered edge thin plancet which in fine condition is very rare. 1798 and 1799 none were coined, but in 1800 the Half-Cent appears but changed in design, similar to that of the

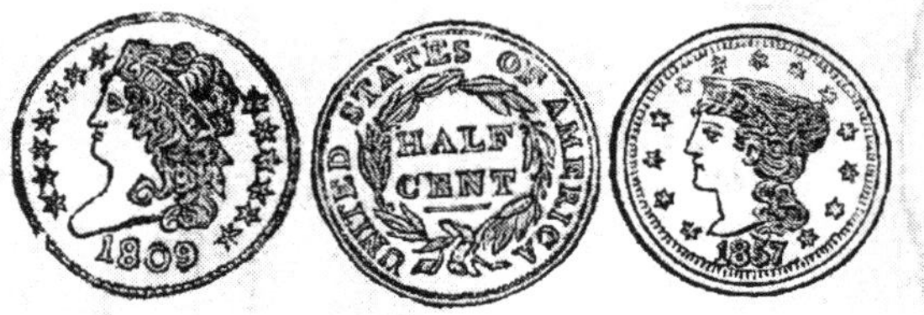
1809
UNITED STATES OF AMERICA
HALF CENT
1857

Cent and the design was continued to 1808 inclusive, none were coined in 1801. The Half-Cent of 1802 in a fine condition is worth a large premium, in 1809 the design was changed to that of the Cent, and coined to 1811 inclusive, when coinage was suspended until 1825, the same devices were used until 1836 inclusive, none were coined in 1827 and 1830, in 1828 one variety has but twelve stars. They again were coined in 1840 with the same pattern of the Cent of that year and continued without intermission until 1857 inclusive where their coinage was discontinued and none have been coined since.

COLONIAL COINS.

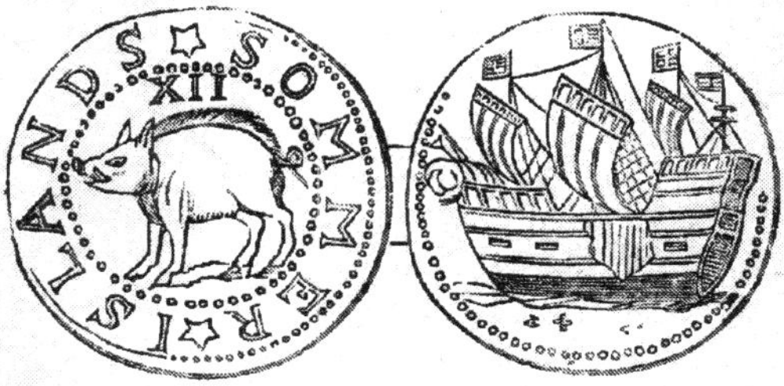
SOMMER ISLANDS
XII

The brass pieces of money, known as the "Sommer Islands" pieces, were undoubtedly the earliest coins ever struck for America. Their date and the history of the coinage is not known, although there is reason to believe that they were current about the year 1616. John Smith, Governor of Virginia, in his history relates that Sir George Somers was shipwrecked upon the Bermudas, or Sommer Islands, in 1612, and that four years later Daniel Tuckar arrived as governor of these Islands. Smith adds that they found a certain kind of brass money in circulation with a "hogge" on one side. It appears that the islands were infested with these brutes. The Sommer Islands Shilling has on one side a hog in the centre with XII above, and both are surrounded with a beaded circle; exterior to and around the latter is the legend "Sommer Islands." On the reverse side is a ship, with canvas spread and a flag on each of her mast-heads; a beaded circle surrounds the exterior of both sides. The Sommer Island sixpence is about half the size of the Shilling, and an

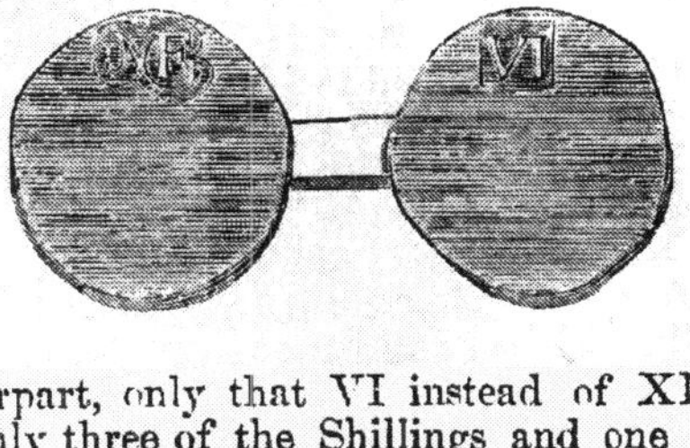

exact counterpart, only that VI instead of XII surmounts the hog. Only three of the Shillings and one Sixpence are known; the former has been imitated.

The New England Shilling, Sixpence, and Threepence were the first silver coins made in America. They were simple thin planchets of silver, having N E stamped into one side, and XII, VI or III stamped into the other side. The authority for the coinage was given in the year 1652. It was shortly after followed by an emission of the Pine Tree money of the same denomination, and the Oak Tree money, which latter also includes a Twopence. On the obverse side is a Pine or Oak Tree in the centre, around this a beaded circle; legend, "Masathvsets in;" on the exterior is another beaded circle. On the reverse, "1652, XII" surrounded by two beaded circles, and between them "New England: An: Dom." Although they were coined for thirty years they all seem to bear the same date, viz., 1652.

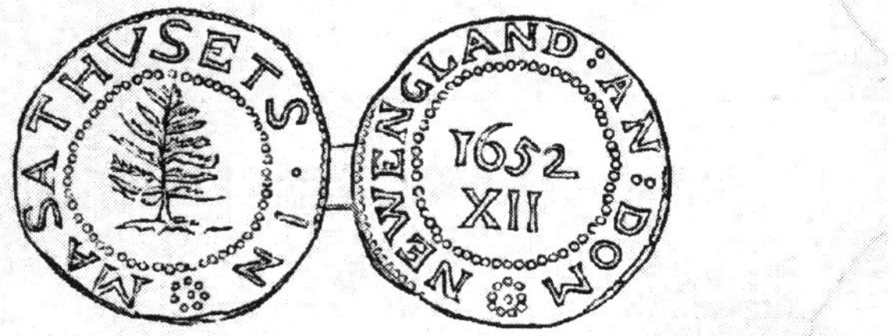
MASATHVSETS IN
NEWENGLAND AN DOM
1652
XII

Copper Coins.—The Granby or Higley coppers are thought to be the first made in America. They were made by a John Higley, at the town of Granby in Connecticut, from 1737 to 1739, inclusive. There are three different varieties of this coin. Their obverses are similar: A deer standing; below him a hand, a star and III; around him is the legend inclosed in two circles, "Value me as you please." The reverse of one

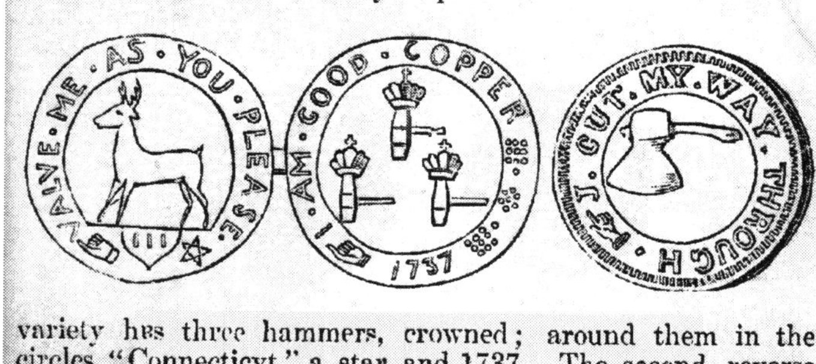
VALVE ME AS YOU PLEASE
III
I AM GOOD COPPER
1737
I CUT MY WAY THROUGH

variety has three hammers, crowned; around them in the circles "Connecticvt," a star and 1737. The second reverse has the three hammers crowned and the legend "I am Good Copper," a hand, some dots fancifully arranged, and 1737. The third variety has a broad-axe and the legend "I Cut my Way Through;" a few also have date 1739. All these varieties of the Granby Copper are quite rare, and when in a satisfactory condition they bring a high price. It is alleged that the fineness of the quality of the copper made them sought after as an alloy of gold, and their use in this way may, in part, account for their present great scarcity.

Among the early American Colonials, the money of Maryland under the Proprietorship of Cecil the second, Lord Baltimore, should not be omitted. Tobacco had been a common medium of exchange; furs were also made use of to some extent, also powder and shot. On one occasion his lordship's cattle were given to some of the soldiers, who had become mutinous for their pay. At a subsequent time a tax was levied upon the people of several of the counties for a particular purpose. To obviate the inconvenience of these media of exchange, the dies for a silver coinage of shillings, sixpence and groats, were prepared in London. A limited number of each was struck, and they are all now rare—the groats much the most so. They each have a bust of Lord Baltimore, draped, looking toward the observer's left. Legend: "Cæcilivs: Dns:

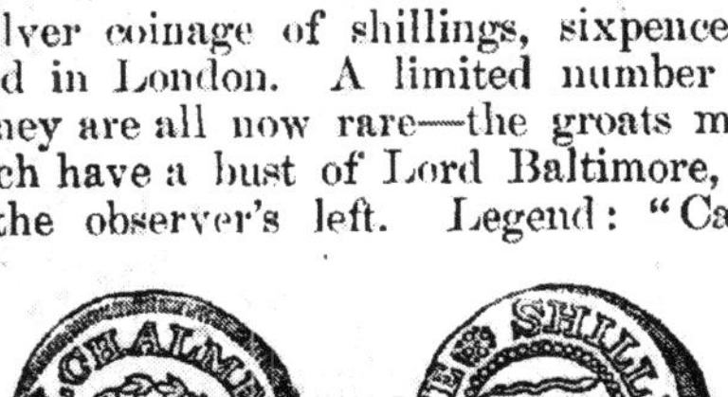

Terræ Mariæ:" etc. Reverse: a lozenged shield, surmounted by a crown, and dividing the numerals XII., VI. and IV. Legend: "Crescite: et: Multiplicamini."

There is also in existence a copper piece, supposed to be unique, and evidently a penny. One side has a similar design with the silver pieces. The reverse has a ducal coronet with two pennants flying. Legend: "Denarivm: Terra Mariæ."

In the year 1783 a goldsmith of Annapolis, Maryland, issued silver tokens of three denominations: shillings, sixpence and threepence. The *shilling* has two hands clasped within a wreath. Legend: "I Chalmers Annapolis." Reverse, a circle is divided by a horizontal bar; above it is a serpent; below it are two doves vis-a-vis, holding a branch in their

beaks. Legend; "One shilling," 1783. The *sixpence* has a five pointed star within a wreath. Legend: "I Chalmers. Annapolis." Reverse; a long cross, two arms terminating in stars and two in crescents; a leaf in each angle. Legend: " I.

C. Sixpence," 1783. The *threepence* has two hands clasped within a wreath. Legend: "I. Chalmers. Annap's." Reverse; a branch encircled by a wreath. Legend: "Three Pence," 1783. The Shilling is rather common; a good one brings three dollars. The Sixpence is rare and sells from six to ten dollars when fine. The groat is scarce and worth eight or ten dollars.

Another private token in silver is sometimes called the Baltimore Town Piece. It has a head facing left in a circle.

Legend: "Baltimore Town, July 4, 1790." Reverse, "Three Pence," within a circle, underscored. Legend: "Standish Barry." The piece brings eight dollars and more.

In 1682, the colonial legislature of New Jersey passed a law legalizing a kind of copper money brought from Ireland by a settler named Mark Newby. There were two sizes, bearing different legends on the reverse. On their obverse, King Charles the First, in the character of King David, appears kneeling and playing upon a harp. Above the harp is a crown with a piece of brass inserted into it, Legend, "Floreat Rex." The larger piece has on the reverse, St. Patrick standing, holding a trefoil or shamrock in his right hand and a crozier in his left. Several people are around him, apparently to receive his blessing. At his left is a shield with the coat of arms of Dublin. Legend, "Ecce Grex."

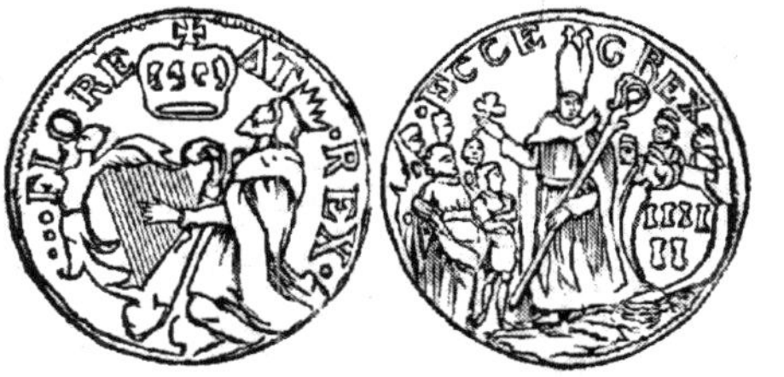
FLORE AT REX
ECCE GREX

The small coin has on its reverse St. Patrick standing, in his left hand a double cross, the right is extended. Snakes and other reptiles are fleeing before him. At the right is a church. Legend, "Quiescat Plebs." A few of the smaller size are found in silver. But in either metal they are very scarce, and usually they are badly worn by circulation.

A token much prized by collectors is known as the Carolina Elephant. The obverse is from a rather common English token known now as the London Elephant. The animal is standing with his head down. There is no legend. Reverse: "God: preserve: Carolina: and the Lords: Proprieters 1694." This is in six lines. One variety spells one word Proprietors, and is of great rarity.

There is also a new England Elephant. Obverse from the same die as the last London piece. "Reverse, "God: Preserve: New: England: 1694," in five lines. Only two or three of these are known at the present time. A very fine one sold in the Mickley collection in 1867 for $235.00. William S. Appleton, of Boston, was the purchaser.

An interesting medalet that passed as money among the colonists is known as the Pitt token. A bust of the orator is circumscribed with the legend, "The Restorer of Commerce

GOD
PRESERVE
CAROLINA AND
THE LORDS
PROPRIETORS
1694

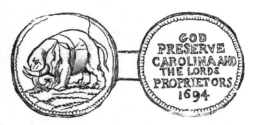

1766: No Stamps." The other side has a ship with canvass spread and five flags flying, sailing towards the observer's right; she is about striking on the word "America," which is placed in a straight line in the right field. Legend: "Thanks

THE·RESTORER OF·COMMERCE 1766: NO·STAMPS:
THANKS TO·THE·FRIENDS·OF·LIBERTY·AND·TRADE·
AMERICA

to the friends of Liberty and Trade." The piece brings from twenty-five cents to five or six dollars, according to condition.

The needs of the colonists for a circulating medium was met in 1722–23 by the issue of the Rosa Americana money.

GEORGIUS·D·G·MAG·BRI·FRA·ET·HIB·REX
ROSA·AMERICANA 1723
UTILE·DULCI

A man named William Wood obtained patents for coining

much used in the latter country. The Rosa's are in a composition according to the terms of the patent, of silver, brass and spelter. The largest piece, usually called the penny, has a head of George I., looking to the right, laureated. Legend; "Georgivs: D: G: Mag: Bri: Fra: et. Hib: Rex." Reverse; a full-blown rose (in some cases surmounted with a crown.) Legend, "Rosa Americana, 1722" (or 1723.) On a scroll below is the sentiment "Utile Dulci." One variety is without the scroll. The half penny is similar; a few are found with the date 1724. The farthing is also similar. The words Utile Dulci are never found on the uncrowned halfpence and farthings. Fine specimens of the Rosa's bring from five to ten dollars each. The rarer varieties, of course, much more.

An extremely rare Rosa Americana of the largest size exists, of the date 1738. One of them is said to be in the British Museum. Another was sold from the collection of Dr. Chas. Clay of Manchester, England, in New York City, in the

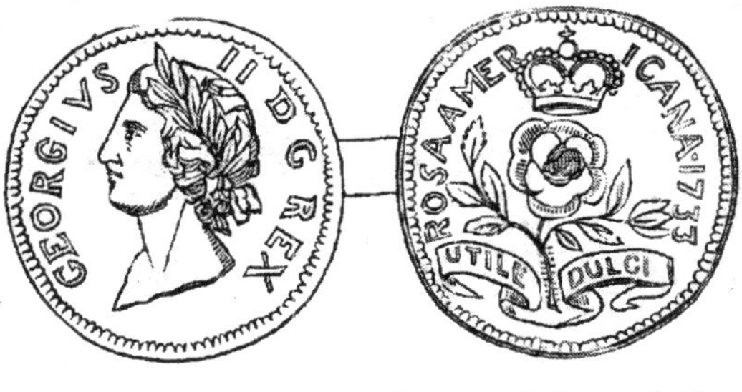
GEORGIVS II D G REX
ROSA AMERICANA 1733
UTILE
DULCI

year 1871, for $190. Obverse, laureated bust of George II. "Georgivs II., D. G. Rex." Reverse, rose branch with seven leaves, a full-blown rose and a bud crowned; "Rosa Americana, 1733." "Utile Dulci," on a scroll, beneath the rose.

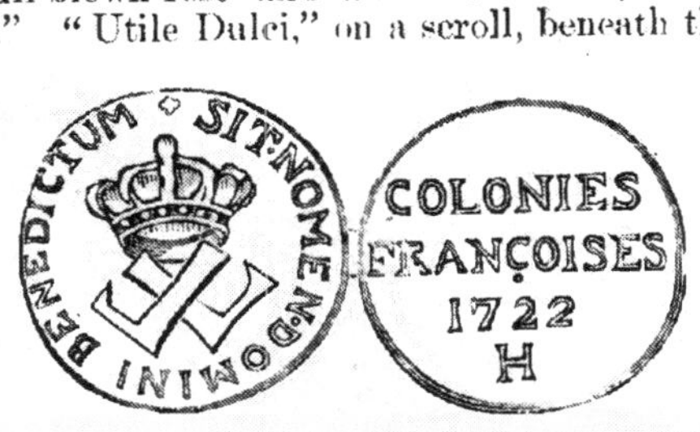
SIT NOMEN DOMINI BENEDICTUM
COLONIES
FRANÇOISES
1722
H

We sometimes meet with a copper coin something smaller in diameter and not so thick as the old U. S. Cent, having the following characters: Obverse, two L's crossed under a crown. Legend, "Sit Nomen Domini Benedictum." Reverse, "Colonies Francoises 1721 H." Sometimes the date is 1722. The piece tells its own story, being issued during the min-

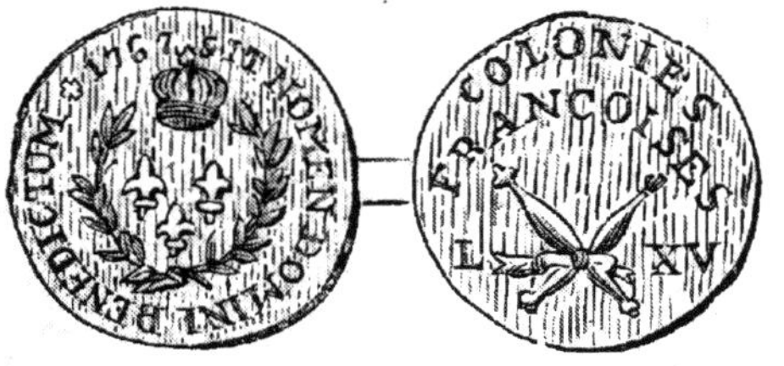
NOMEN DOMINI BENEDICTUM
COLONIES FRANCOISES
L XV

ority of Louis XV by the French Government for its Colonies. As Louisiana was one of these, it probably circulated there, and is accordingly classed among American Colonials.

Another considerably heavier copper, engrailed on the edge, was issued by the same government in the year 1767. Obverse: Two flambeaux, crossed and tied together. Legend: "Colonies Francoises L. XV." Reverse: Three fleur-de-lis under a crown, are encircled by two half-wreaths fastened by their stems. Legend, "Sit Nomen Domini Benedictum 1767."

The majority of those now seen have had the three fleur-de-lis, obliterated by the letters R F stamped upon them. This, it is believed, was done by order of the Republican Government after its establishment.

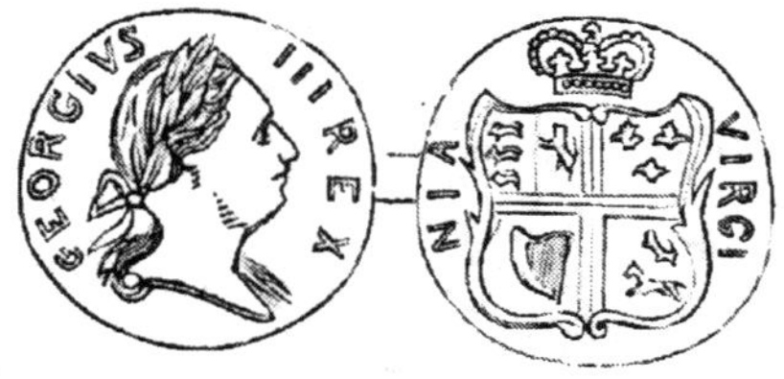
GEORGIVS III REX
VIRGI NIA

The well-known Virginia Half Pennies seem to have been very plentiful. A number of different dies were used. A laureated bust of George the Third is surrounded, as on the English half penny, with his title, "Georgivs. III. Rex." The reverse has an ornamental and crowned shield, emblazoned quarterly: 1, England empaling Scotland; 2, France; 3, Ireland; 4, the electoral dominions. Legend: "Virginia." Date,

1773. One variety is so much larger than the others as sometimes to be called the penny, but it is not nearly large enough.

A similar device, dated 1774, has been found in silver, and is known as the Virginia shilling. It is possible that a coinage of shillings for Virginia was intended at this time, of which the above was a pattern. However this may have been, the coin is of great rarity, probably less than half a dozen in all are known to coin collectors of the present day.

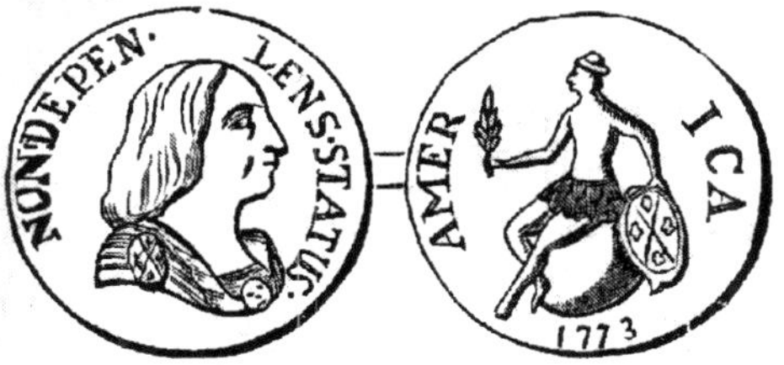
NONDEPEN·DENS·STATUS·
AMER ICA
1773

A very rare if not unique piece, whose history is not known, is called the "Non Dependens Status," from the legend on the obverse. This legend surrounds a draped bust, facing right, the hair falling on the shoulder. Reverse, an Indian in a tunic of feathers, facing left, seated on a globe. In his right hand is a bunch of tobacco; his left rests upon a shield. Legend, "America." Date, 1778. Judging by the copy that has been made of this piece, which is said to have been engraved only, it must be a fine design handsomely executed.

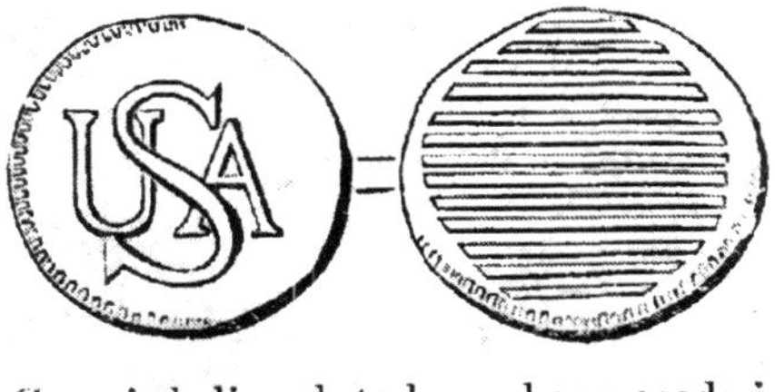
USA

The Bar Cent is believed to have been made in England, in the year 1785, and sent over to New York for circulation in America. It has the monogram U. S. A. in large Roman letters. In one variety the S is over the other letters, and in another the S is over the U, and the A over the S. The reverse has thirteen parallel bars. A good Bar Cent can be had for three or four dollars. Other pieces made probably in this country, but not authorized, that were intended for the needs of the New York colonists, will now be described.

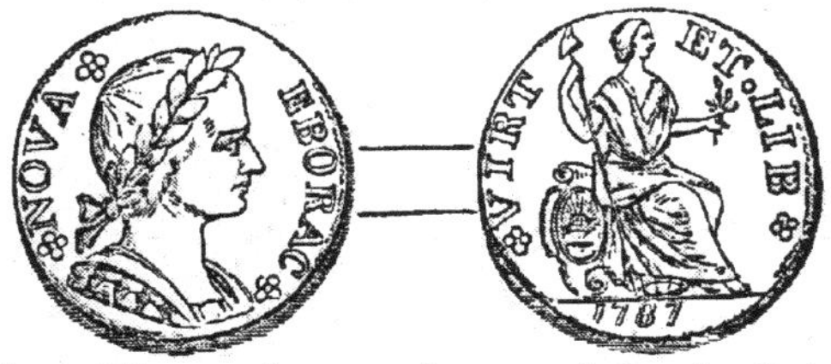
NOVA EBORAC
VIRT ET. LIB
1787

The Nova Eboracs have a laureated head, facing right, with mailed bust. Legend, "Nova Eborac." Reverse, the Goddess of Liberty, seated upon a globe; in one variety facing right, in three others facing left. She holds the liberty pole with a cap. in the right hand, and an olive branch in the left, Beside her is the New York shield. Legend, "Virt. et Lib." Date, 1787. The common varieties bring, in good condition, about a dollar.

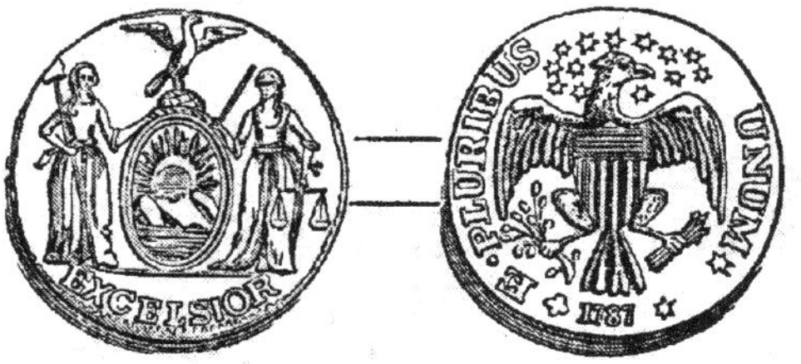
EXCELSIOR
E. PLURIBUS UNUM.
1787

The Excelsior coppers have the coat of arms of the State of New York, with the word "Excelsior" in the exergue. Reverse, an eagle displayed; on the breast a shield argent; in one talon a bundle of arrows, in the other an olive branch and thirteen stars about his head. Date, 1787. Two varieties; in good condition, fifteen to twenty dollars.

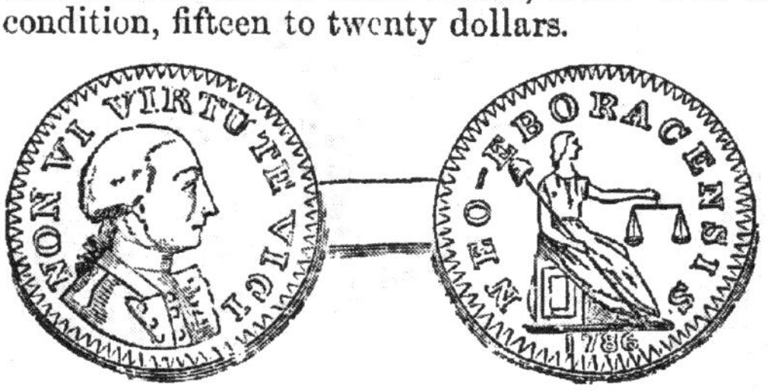
NON VI VIRTUTE VICI.
NEO-EBORACENSIS
1786

The New York Washington Cent has a bust with wig, and with military draping, face right. Legend, "Non vi virtute vici." Reverse, the Goddess of Liberty, seated, with liberty pole and scales of justice. Legend, "Neo Eboracensis." Date, 1786.

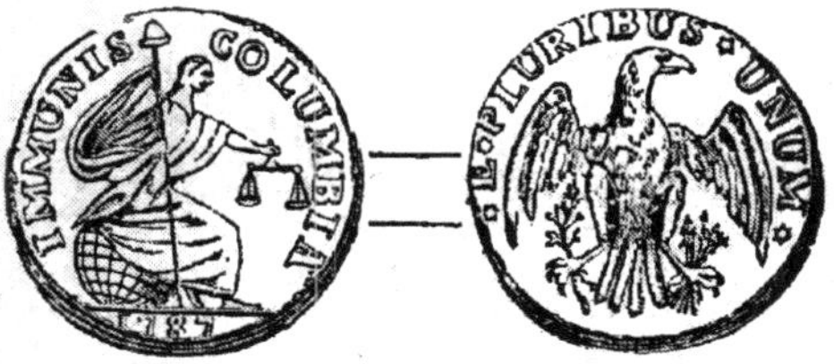
IMMUNIS COLUMBIA
1787
E PLURIBUS UNUM

The New York Immunis Columbia has the Goddess of Liberty, seated upon a globe, the scales in her left hand, and liberty pole, with cap and flag, in the right. Legend, "Immunis Columbia." Date, 1787. Reverse: An eagle displayed. with arrows and olive branch in his talons. Legend, " E Pluribus Unum."

The George Clinton Copper has the bust of Governor Clinton facing right, with legend "George Clinton." Reverse, the State arms of New York, and in the exergue "1787 Excelsior." This last reverse is found also combined with the Liber Natus, which has an Indian standing. facing left, with tomahawk in the right hand and bow in the left, a bundle of

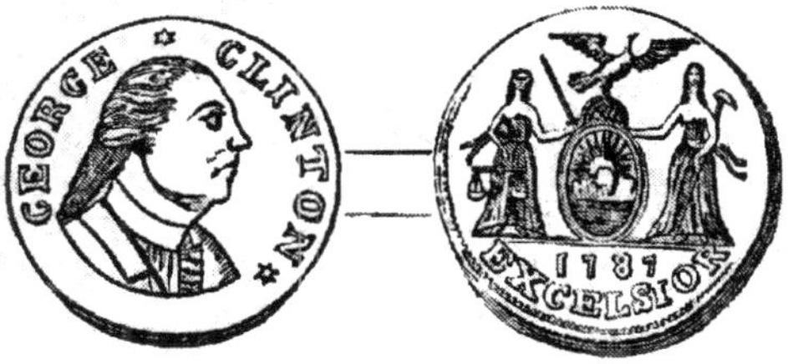
GEORGE CLINTON
1787
EXCELSIOR

arrows also at his back. Legend, "Liber Natus Libertatem Defendo." This latter obverse is also found combined with another reverse, as follows: An eagle stands upon a section of the globe. Legend, "Neo Emboracus 1787 Excelsior." The foregoing are very rare, excepting the Immunis Columbia, Which sells in good condition for five dollars or more. The others, including the N. Y. Washington, bring from twenty-five to more than a hundred dollars.

Brashers's Doubloon has the device, a sun rising from behind a range of mountains, in the foreground the sea, "Brasher" underneath, and a beaded circle around. Reverse, an eagle displayed with shield upon his breast, and arrows

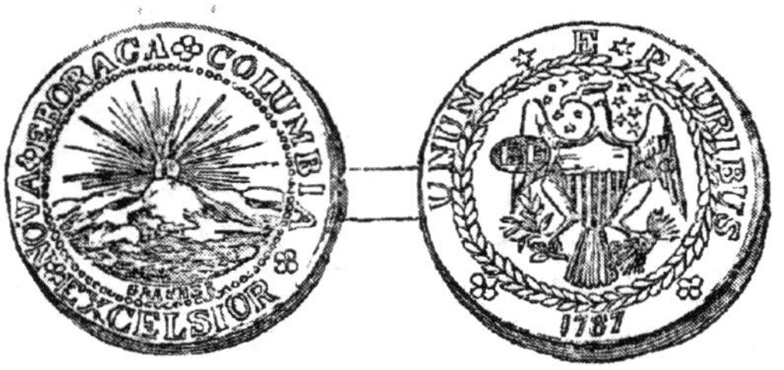
NOVA EBORACA COLUMBIA EXCELSIOR
UNUM E PLURIBUS
1787

and olive branch in his talons; thirteen stars about his head. "E. B.," in an oval has been struck in his right wing. Legend: "Unum E Pluribus 1787." Only about four of the gold pieces are known, one of them in the U. S. Mint cabinet.

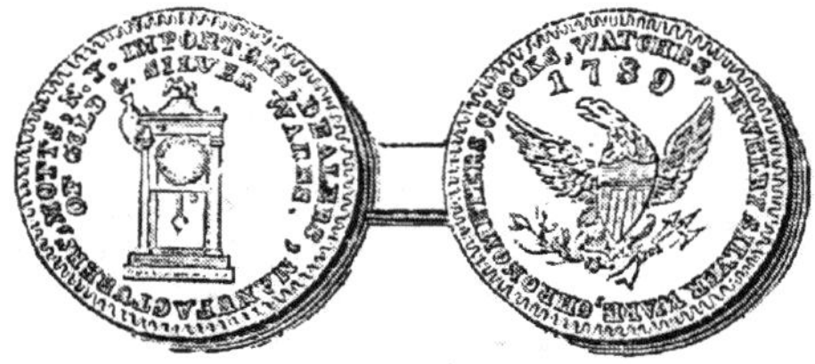
1789

The Mott tokens were issued by the Mott firm in N. Y. city, and are considered the first tradesmen's tokens coined in America. Device, a clock with an eagle perched upon the top. Legend, "Motts, N. Y. Importers, Dealers, Manufacturers of Gold and Silver Wares." Reverse, an eagle with wings expanded, facing left; a shield is upon his breast, and the talons have arrows and olive branch respectively. Above is the date, 1789. Legend: "Chronometers, Clocks. Watches, Jewelry, Silver Ware."

The Talbot, Allum & Lee Tokens have as device a ship sailing towards the right. Above the ship, "New York." Legend: "Talbot, Allum & Lee, One Cent." Reverse, the Goddess of Liberty, standing beside a bale of merchandise; her right hand supports the liberty staff, with cap; her left rests upon a rudder. Legend, "Liberty and commerce." Date, 1794, On the edge. "Payable at the store of."

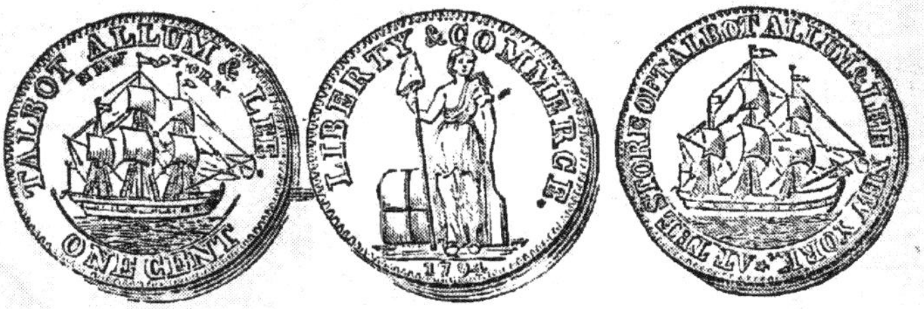
TALBOT ALLUM & LEE
NEW YORK
ONE CENT
LIBERTY & COMMERCE
1794
AT THE STORE OF TALBOT ALLUM & LEE NEW YORK

In 1795 there was a slight variation, reading as follows on the obverse: "At the store of Talbot, Allum & Lee, New York." On the edge, "We promise to pay the bearer One Cent." Of course the date was 1795.

The tokens of Mott and of Talbot, Allum & Lee are quite plentiful. That of the latter of 1795 is scarcer than the 1794. From one to two dollars will purchase any of the three, in fine condition.

In the year 1785 permission was given to Reuoen Harman, Jr., of Vermont, by the Legislature of that State, to coin copper money. In the latter part of the year they first appeared, and were coined in 1786, 7 and 8. The first bore the following devices: a sun rising behind a wooded range of hills, beneath it a plow. Legend, "Vermonts Res Publica" on one variety and Vermontis Res Publica" on another. Reverse, an eye with a small circle, surrounded with twenty-six rays, one-half of each being longer than the alternate half. A circle of thirteen stars fills up the spaces between the end of the short rays and the long ones. Legend, "Stella Quarta Decima."

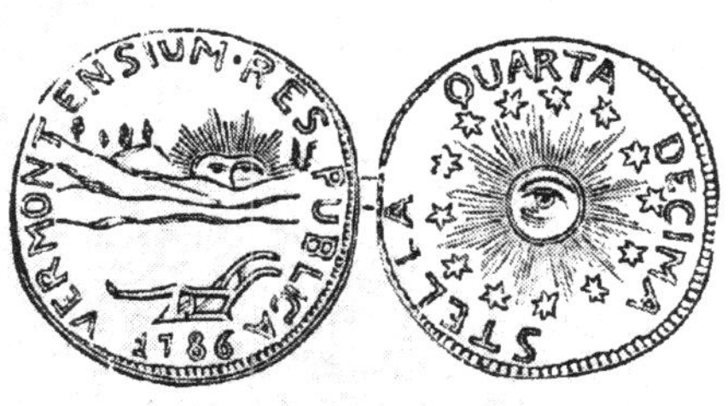
VERMONTENSIUM·RES PUBLICA
1786
QUARTA DECIMA STELLA

In 1786 a similar style was adopted on one variety, but the legend reads "Vermontensium Res Publica." On the reverse the long rays terminate in sharp points, and the others are omitted

Another variety was totally different. It has a laureated bust, facing right, with the legend, "Auctori Vermon." Reverse, the Goddess of Liberty seated, facing left, with staff and olive branch. Legend, "Inde et Lib." This is called the Baby-head Vermont, and is valued at from 50 cents to $2.00, according to condition.

The third variety has the head facing left, and is rather scarce.

In 1787 the head faces in two varieties toward the right, and in one toward the left; the legend on the reverse of the latter is "Britannia." It is common.

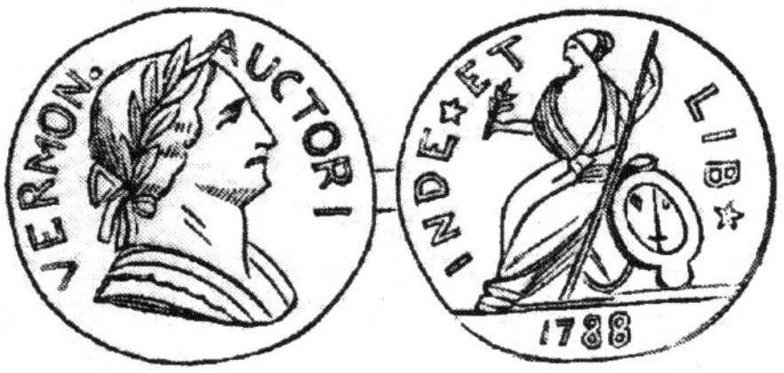
VERMON. AUCTORI
INDE ET LIB
1788

In all the issues of 1788 the head faces right. There are a number of varieties, some common and others rare.

There is a rare Vermont, bearing for reverse an Immunis Columbia," exactly like that described on page 98, excepting that it is dated 1785, and the legend reads "Immune Columbis." In good condition it is worth five dollars.

The Tory Cents are of two kinds; one of these has the reverse "Immune Columbia," the other has that of the ordinary Vermont coppers of 1788. The obverses are similar to the English half-pence of the period, having a laureated bust of George III, with his title, "Georgivs III., Rex."

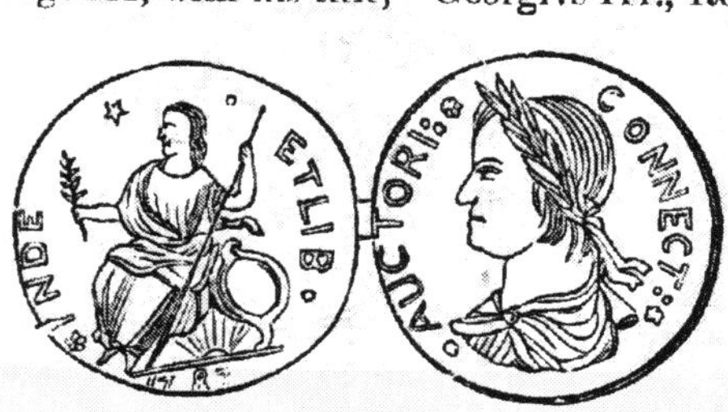
INDE ETLIB.
AUCTORI: CONNECT:

Authority was given, in 1785, to Samuel Bishop, James Hillhouse, Joseph Hopkins and John Goodrich, to coin coppers for Connecticut. The dies were made by Abel Buel of New Haven. They were coined in the period from 1785 to 1788 inclusive, and are similar to those of Vermont of 1788, excepting that the legend is "Auctori Connec." In each year, different varieties have the head facing right in some cases and left in others. The most noteworthy of the Connecticut's are, the African head of 1785, the "Et Lib Inde," and Hercules head of 1786; the "Et Lib Inde," Governor Bradford head, Horned bust, Laughing head, Connect, Auctobi, Auctopi, and Auciori of 1787; and the Conlec of 1788. The most of these are not rare and can usually be had in very good condition for a dollar or less.

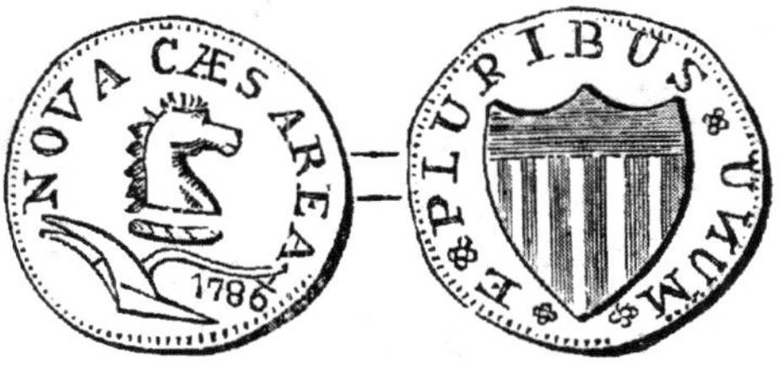
NOVA CÆSAREA
1786
E PLURIBUS UNUM

The coining of coppers for New Jersey was given by law to Walter Mould, Thomas Goadsby and Albion Cox. There were two Mints, one at Elizabethtown and one at Morristown. They have a horse head, usually facing right, with a plow below it, and the legend "Nova Cæsarea." Date in the exergue. Reverse, a shield with the motto around the border "E Pluribus unum." In ordiuary condition, the New Jersey can be had for from ten to fifty cents. The most popular varieties are:

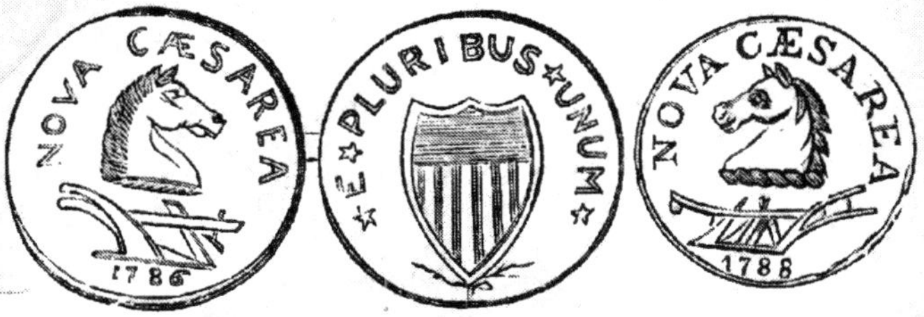
NOVA CÆSAREA
1786
E PLURIBUS UNUM
NOVA CÆSAREA
1788

Plow without coulter, ...	$1 00 to 3 00
Plow with date under the beam, ...	$100 00
Plow with Immunis Columbia, 1786, for obverse,	50 00

Plow with Gen. Washington bust	" "	150 00
E Pluribs Unum, ...	$2 00 to	4 00
Horse head facing left, ...	1 00 to	5 00
With a fox or horse on the reverse, . .	1 00 to	4 00

Dr. E. Maris of Philadelphia, has published a history of the coins of New Jersey, with a large phototype plate of the obverses and reverses of all known varieties. They are of the natural size and make 140 pictures.

Massachusstts coined cents and half-cents, each dated 1787 and 1788. They are similar in design, having an Indian standing, with a bow in his right and an arrow in his left hand. Legend, "Commonwealth," separated by a five-pointed star. Reverse, and eagle displayed, on his breast a shield argent, six pales gules, a chief azure; on the chief the word

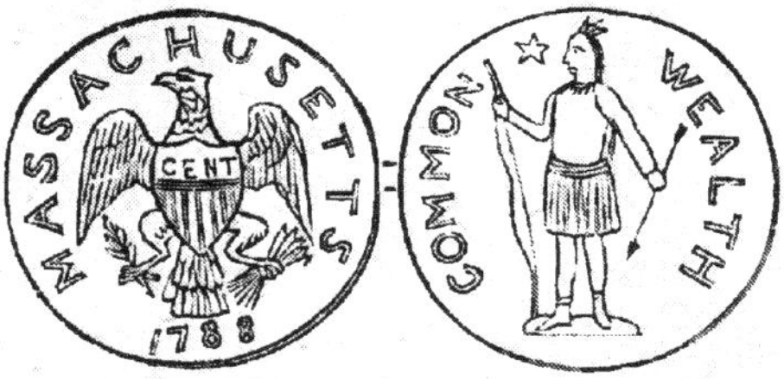
MASSACHUSETTS
CENT
1788
COMMON
WEALTH

"Cent" or "Half-Cent"; in the eagle's right talon is an olive branch and in his left a bundle of arrows. Legend, "Massachusetts." Date in the exergue. The cent is worth a dollar in fine condition, the half-cent twice as much as the cent.

There are several pieces in silver, of patterns designed for the Colonies, which are of two sizes. They have an eye in the centre, surrounded with 13 rays and 13 stars between the points, similar to the reverse of the Vermontensium pieces. Legend, "Nova Constellatio." Reverse, a wreath encircles "U. S. 1000" on the large and "U. S. 500" on the smaller piece. Legend, "Libertas Justitia," and the date 1783 in the exergue. One variety of the smaller-sized piece is without date or legend on the reverse. All are extremely rare or unique.

The copper Nova Constellatios are similar in design to the silver pieces above described. One variety has wedge-shaped blocks, pointing towards the centre, between each of the stars. Another has the legend spelled "Nova Constelatio." Some varieties have, on the reverse, Roman and

LIBERTAS ET JUSTITIA · 1785 ·
CONSTELLATIO
NOVA

others script letters in the centre (U. S.,) but none have the denominational figures like the silver pieces. They have various dates, 1783, 1785 and 1786. The latter are exceedingly rare, the others are all common. Some rare combinations are, with "Immune Columbia" 1785 reverse, worth fifteen or twenty dollars, and the same with the wedge-shaped rays and "Immune Columbia" reverse, lately sold for one hundred dollars.

CONSTELLATIO
NOVA
IMMUNE COLUMBIA
1785

Of the "Inimica Tyrannis" coppers there are two slight variations in the obverse. An Indian is standing before an altar with his right foot upon a crown. In his left hand is a bow, in the right an arrow, and a quiver full of arrows on his back, Legend, "Inimica Tyrannis Americana." There are two reverses. In each there is a cluster of thir-

INIMICA TYRANNIS
AMERICANA
CONFEDERATIO
1785

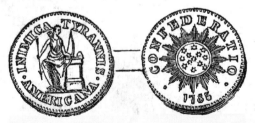

teen stars in the centre, with a glory surrounding them, in one case having twenty-four and in the other sixteen rays.

Legend, "Confederatio." Date 1785. Both obverses are combined with the first-named reverse, and one of them with both reverses. The reverse "Confederatio," is also combined with a reverse "Nova Constellatio" 1785, with the Gen. Washington head mentioned in the coins of New Jersey, with the "Immunis Columbia" 1786, and with a reverse similar to that on the Excelsior cent described on page 98, excepting that it is dated 1786.

IMMUNIS COLUMBIA.
1786
CONFEDERATIO
1785

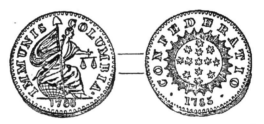

The last-named die is also found with the Gen. Washington and with that, the N. J. shield, which is an obverse to the "Immunis Columbia" of 1786.

Washington Tokens.—There are in existence a large number of copper and silver pieces having a bust of Washington on one side. Only those tokens that were issued for or were used as money will be described here, all others being properly medals or medalets.

WASHINGTON & INDEPENDENCE
1783
STATES OF AMERICA
ONE
CENT

The Unity States Cent has a bust of Washington, draped and facing left. Legend, "Washington and Independence, 1783." Reverse, "One Cent" in two lines, enclosed by two olive branches, fastened at the bottom with a ribbon. Legend, "Unity States of America." This is supposed to be of French origin.

A similar obverse is found combined with a different reverse, having Liberty seated looking left, with pole and cap on it in the left hand, and with an olive branch in the right hand, which is extended. Legend, "United States" above. There were two dies of this variety; one pair of them still exists in England, and proof-impressions are furnished from them, some in silver and others in copper; the latter has an engrailed line on the edge to distinguish it from original impressions.

Two other dies have smaller heads on their obverses; they are known as the *Small Head Washington*, those last previously described are known as the *Large Head Washington.*

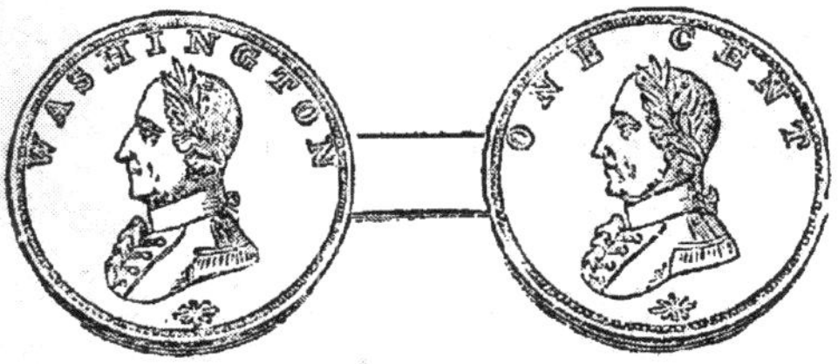
WASHINGTON
ONE CENT

The *Double Head Washington* has a small head on both obverse and reverse. The former has the legend "Washington"; the latter the legend "One Cent."

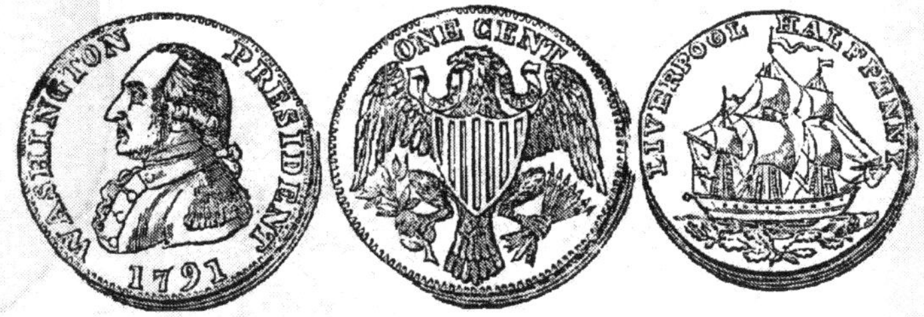
WASHINGTON PRESIDENT
1791
ONE CENT
LIVERPOOL HALFPENNY

The *large Eagle Washington Cent* has a bust of Washington in military costume, facing left, the hair tied in a queue; date 1791; legend, "Washington President." Reverse, a large eagle displayed, on his breast a shield argent, six pales gules; in his beak is a scroll bearing the motto, "E Pluribus Unum"; in his right talon is an olive branch, in the left a bundle of arrows; above the head are the words, "One Cent;" on the edge are the words, "United States of America."

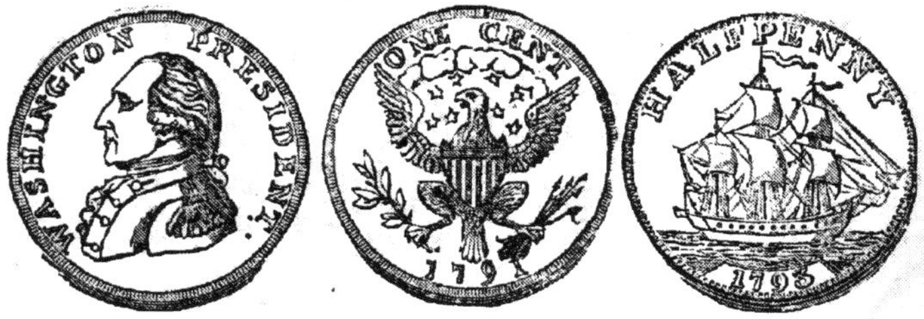
WASHINGTON PRESIDENT.
ONE CENT
HALFPENNY
1793

The *small eagle Washington Cent* is precisely like the large eagle cent on the obverse, excepting that the date is wanting. The reverse has a smaller eagle than the last, displayed, with the wings upraised and the talons grasping the olive branch and arrows; a shield on the breast is similar to that on the large eagle Cent excepting that it has a Chief azure. The words "One Cent" are above and the date 1791, at the base; a circle of clouds extends from wing to wing of the eagle, and eight stars are about his head. The edge is lettered "United States of America."

The last described obverse is found with another reverse, which has a ship with canvas spread, sailing toward the light; above it is the legend "Halfpenny;" the date is 1793.

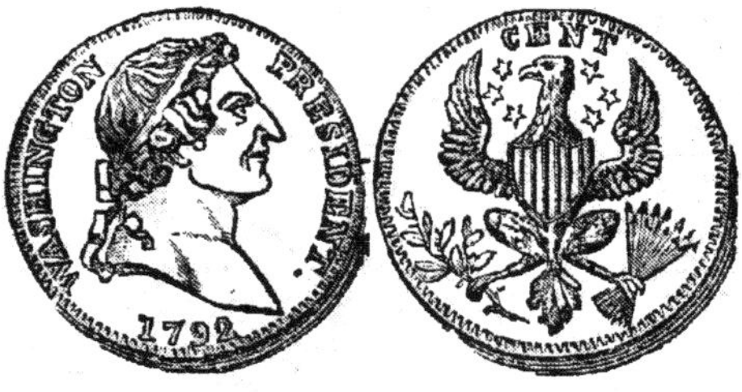
WASHINGTON PRESIDENT.
1792
CENT

The *naked bust Washington Cent* has the undraped bust of Washington facing right, the hair tied with a fillet, date 1792. The reverse is similar to the small eagle Cent, excepting that the date is wanting, also the clouds, and there are six instead of eight stars.

All the forgoing Washington pieces excepting the first-described are of English origin. The next are from dies supposed to have been made in Philadelphia, by Peter Getz of Lancaster, Penna.

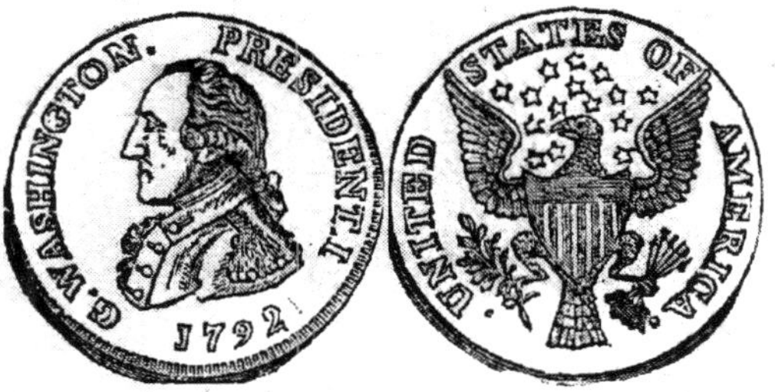
G. WASHINGTON. PRESIDENT. I.
1792
UNITED STATES OF AMERICA

The 1792 *Washington Cent and Half-Dollar* resemble on the obverse the large eagle Cent, excepting the date 1792 instead of 1791, and the legend which reads "G. Washington President I." The reverse resembles that of the small eagle Cent, excepting that there are fifteen stars instead of eight; the clouds are wanting and the body of the eagle is larger in the 1792 piece. When in copper this is called the *Cent;* when in silver the *Half-Dollar.* They are larger in diameter than the other Washington Cents.

The next described pieces are of unknown origin.

The *Washington piece with stars over the eagle* resembles the large eagle Cent of 1791, excepting that on the obverse the date is 1792, and the reverse, in place of the words "One Cent," there is a single star over the head of the eagle, above which twelve similar stars form a curve reaching from wing to wing of the eagle. It is found in copper and in silver; some specimens have the edge lettered "United States of America."

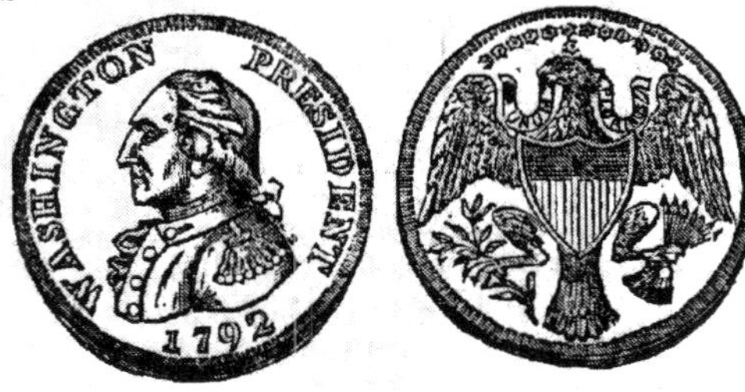
WASHINGTON PRESIDENT
1792

The following token is supposed to be of American origin.

A bust of Washington with queue, facing right; legend, "George Washington." Reverse, an eye in the centre, with rays radiating around it, every third ray being longer than the rest and separated from each other, fifteen stars arranged in a circle; legend, "Success to the United States." It is

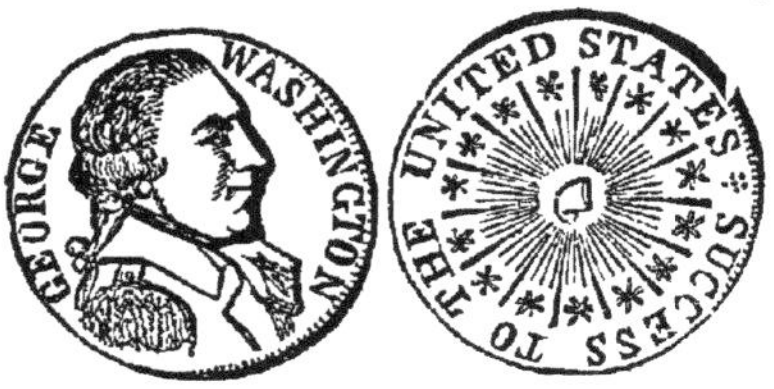
GEORGE WASHINGTON
SUCCESS TO THE UNITED STATES

usually in brass, but rarely it is found in copper, and is of two sizes, the larger, something larger than the early U. S. Quarters, the other a shade larger than the early Dimes.

A few English tokens, usually classed as Colonials, referring to this country, will now be mentioned.

The Georgivs Triumpho copper has a head laureated, facing right. Legend, "Georgivs Triumpho." Reverse, Goddess of Liberty, facing left, behind a frame of thirteen bars with a fleur-de-lis in each corner. An olive branch is held in her right hand, a staff of liberty in her left. Legend, "Voce Popoli," Date 1783. Worth a dollar in fine condition.

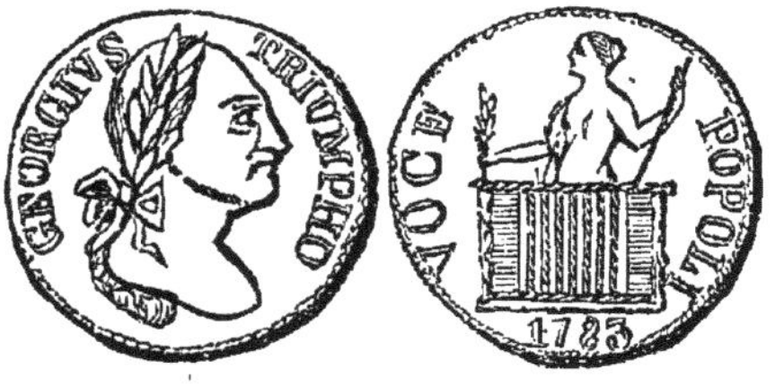
GEORGIVS TRIUMPHO
VOCE POPOLI
1783

The North American Token has a female seated, facing left, with a harp. Legend, "North American Token." Date 1781. Reverse, a ship sailing to the left. Legend, Commerce." Worth fifty cents when fine.

The Auctori Plebis has a bust, laureated and draped, facing left. Legend, "Auctori: Plebis." Reverse, a female seated, with her left arm resting on an anchor, the right on a globe; at her feet is a lion. Legend, "Indep. et liber." Date 1787. Worth one to three dollars.

The Franklin Press has an old-fashioned printing press and legend "Sic oritur doctrina surgetque libertas." Date 1794. Reverse, Payable at the Franklin Press, London," in five straight lines. Worth fifty cents in fine condition.

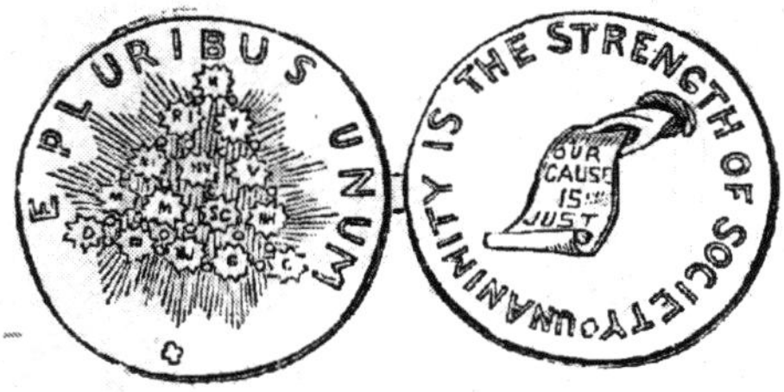
E PLURIBUS UNUM
UNANIMITY IS THE STRENGTH OF SOCIETY
OUR CAUSE IS JUST

A popular token, known as the Kentucky Cent, has a hand holding a scroll inscribed "Our Cause is Just." Legend, "Unanimity is the Strength of Society." Reverse, a radiant pyramid, triangular in shape, of fifteen stars united by rings, each star having placed in it the initial of a State, Kentucky being at the top. Legend, "E Pluribus Unum." It is often found considerably circulated, showing it to have been used, and sells for from fifty cents to several dollars, according to condition.

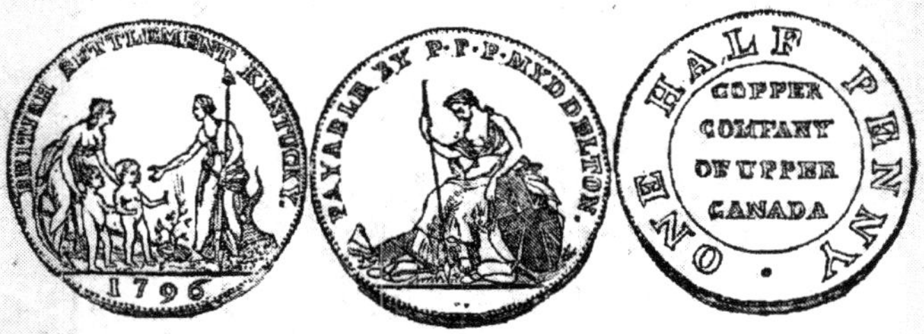
BRITISH SETTLEMENT KENTUCKY.
1796
PAYABLE BY P·P·P·MYDDELTON.
ONE HALF PENNY
COPPER
COMPANY
OF UPPER
CANADA

Two other Kentucky tokens of beautiful execution, which do not appear to have ever circulated, are sometimes brought over from England. They have the same obverse, which has for a device a female, personating Hope, bending before an anchor and presenting two children to a female who stands with a liberty cap in the right hand and with the other outstretched to receive them. Legend, "British Settlement Kentucky." Date 1796. *Reverse No.* 1, Britannia with bowed head, holding a spear inverted; a fasces, broken sword and scales of justice lie at her feet; before her is a cap of liberty. Legend, "Payable by P. P. P. Myddleton." *Reverse No.* 2, "Copper Company of Upper Canada," in four straight lines within a wreath, is surrounded with the legend "One Half Penny." Both of these tokens are found in copper with the first described reverse. It is sometimes found in silver.

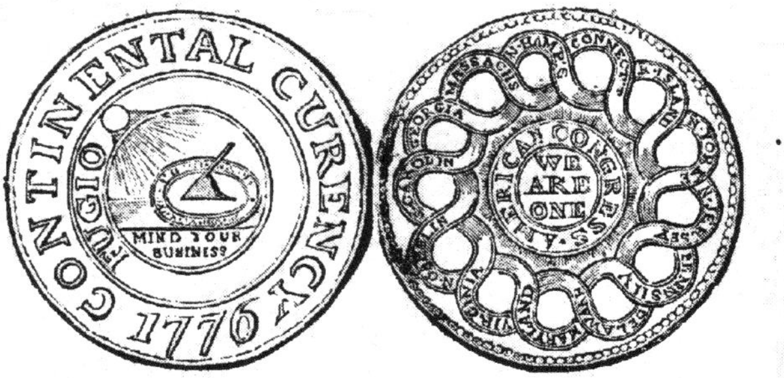
CONTINENTAL CURRENCY
1776
FUGIO
MIND YOUR BUSINESS
AMERICAN CONGRESS
WE ARE ONE

The Continental Currency piece has thirteen rings linked together, each bearing the name of a State, Legend, American Congress," on a label around the centre. In the centre are the words "We are One." Between the legend and rings a circle of rays are seen. Reverse, a sun-dial with the sun shining upon it on the left side. Legend, "Continental Currency." Date 1776 below. "Mind Your Business" below the dial; "Fugio" near the sun and under "Continental."

These pieces are as large as a silver dollar and are usually in tin, but a few are known in silver and one in brass. One variety has currency spelt with one "r" and another, which is rare, has "E. G., Fecit," at the base of the inner circle. The common variety brings about two dollars.

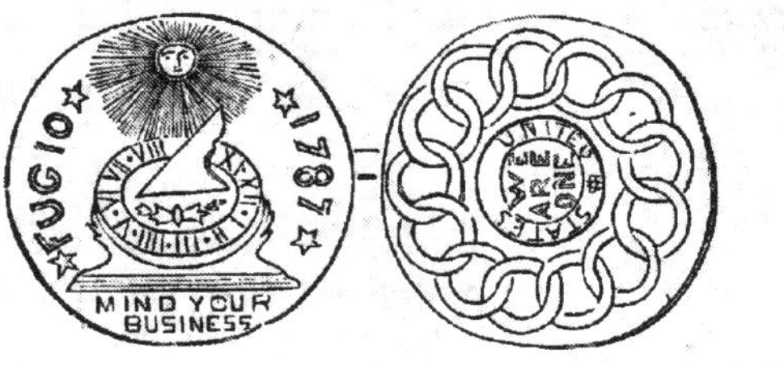
FUGIO
1787
MIND YOUR BUSINESS
UNITED STATES
WE ARE ONE

One of the most interesting and most widely circulated of all the Colonial series remains to be described. They are called the Fugios or Franklin Cents and are the earliest coins issued by authority of the United States. They are all dated 1787, and are made in conformity with the following resolution of Congress, dated July 6, 1787:

"*Resolved*, That the Board of Treasury direct the contractor for the copper coinage to stamp on one side of each piece the following devices, viz.: Thirteen circles linked together, a small circle in the middle, with the words 'United States' round it and in the centre the words 'We are One'; on the other side of the same piece the following device, viz.: A dial with the hours expressed on the face of it; a meridian sun above, on one side of which is to be the word 'Fugio' and on the other the year in figures '1787'; below the dial the words 'Mind Your Business.'"

Great numbers of these pieces were coined, and yet they bring, in perfect condition, seventy-five cents to one dollar. A number of dies were made, varying slightly. In some cases the word "States" preceded "United."

A number of impressions in silver and also in alloy of copper and zinc, from original dies, were struck a few years ago.

There are also a few pieces in existence that differ more widely from those authorized by the resolution of Congress. One of these has stars within the rings, others have the names of the States on the rings, with 'the words "We are One" omitted and "American Congress" taking the place of "United States." Some of them have an eye in the centre, and all of them rays between the motto and the rings. The obverse is without any letters. One specimen is known in brass, and five of different patterns in silver. They all would command high prices, those in silver especially so, but have rarely passed hands.

STANDARD AMERICAN NUMISMATIC PUBLICATIONS.

Monograph of U. S. Cents and Half Cents. 9 Heliotype plates with a hundred of illustrations by Ed. Frossard, very complete. Price $3.00.

Coins of New Jersey, an excellent work by Ed. Maris, M. D. Price $4.00. Illustrated.

The early Coins of America and Laws governing their issue. Illustrations of over 1000 coins on heliotype plate and wood cuts. Most complete work ever published, by Sylvester S. Crosby. Price $12.00.

Current Gold and Silver Coins of all Nations, by Ivan C. Michels, Ph. D. M. A. Illustrations of 1453 foreign coins, their value in U. S. Money A valuable assistant to merchants and bankers and no library is complete without it. Price $3.00. The above works you can get only from all Numismatists or the publishers of this work.

The Coin Collectors Illustrated Guide. 5 numbers are now publishde; it is an assistant to the coin collectors. Per number 15 cents or 2 differerent numbers for 25 cents. Address: P. O. Box 1954. Philadelphia.

U. S. Silver Coin Type Table, by John M. Hazeltine, of all known varieties of dollars, halves and quarters, most complete ever published. Their numismatic value and the prices they sold for onNov. 28th, 29th, 30th, 1881. Price 75 cents.

RARE U. S. COINS.

The rarest United States Coin is the Double Eagle of 1849, of which there is only one in existence and belongs to the U. S. Mint Cabinet. The next in rarity is the Half Eagle of 1815, of this date there are only seven specimens known to exist.

The Silver Dollar of 1804 is also one of the rare coins; of this Dollar only ten genuine pieces are known to exist, all of which are now held by collectors· Of the 1804 Dollar several re-strikes have been made. To obtain a fine one from original die would cost at least $1,000; there is many altered dates. The Half Dollars of 1796 and 1797, if in fine condition bring $40, of the two the 1796 is the rarer and usually sells at a still higher rate.

The Quarter Dollars of 1823 and 1827, if in good condition sell readily at $30 each; but if in strictly fine preservation double that sum is cheerfully paid.

Of the Dimes there are none of extreme rarity, still among the rare coins of this denomination that of 1804 is the rarest, and if in good-condition can be bought at from $5.00 to $10; but a real fine specimen would bring a great deal more.

Among the Half Dimes that of 1802 is the rarest, and a very fine piece with that date sells readily at $100.

Still, there are other United States coins which are much sought after, and as they pass from hand to hand only for their face value, and the collector of coins is always in search of many of them, we think it but right to inform our readers of their nature. To understand well the premium value of any coins of rarity, the condition of the piece is essential. A coin brilliant as if fresh from the coining press is consideede and known as "*proof;*" again, one which is free from the uses and abuses of circulated money is known as "*uncirculated*" and becomes next in premium value. The age of a coin is not always a guarantee of a premium above face value, hence it would be advisable to the readers of this book to suggest to them that a correspondence with a Numismatist of respectability and responsibility is of great importance and will be of benefit to holders of the following coins, which are sold at a premium or advance over face value.

The following prices quoted are meant in good condition, worn condition less and finer a great deal more.

U. S. SILVER DOLLARS.

1804, $500; 1794, 1838, 39, 51, 52, each $20; 1858, $10; 1798, small Eagle 15 stars, $6; 1798, small Eagle, $3; 1836, $3.50; 1799, five stars facing, $2; 1854, 55, 56, $2; 1795, 96, 97, 1801, 02, 03, $1.50 each. · Trade dollars of 1879, 80, 81, and 82 are very rare, as only a few hundred of each as proofs for collectors were struck, and command a premium.

HALF DOLLARS.

All must be in good condition. 1794, $3; 1796, $25; 1797, $20; 1801, $2; 1802, $3; 1815, $2.50; 1836, Reeded or unlettered edge, $1.50; 1838, with an O over the date, $10; 1852, if in good condition, $2.

QUARTER DOLLARS.

1823 and 1827, $20 each; 1853, without sun rays back of eagle and no arrows near date, $4: 1796 and 1804, $2 each.

DIMES.

Of 1804 are worth $5 each; those of 1796, 1797, 1798, 1800, 1801, 1802, 1803 and 1822, if in good condition, are worth $1 to $2, each; those of 1805, 1807, 1809, 1811 and 1846, if in good condition, are worth 50c. to 75c. each.

HALF DIMES.

1802 are worth, if in good condition, $50 each; 1794, 1796, 1797, 1800, 1, 3 and 5, if in good condition, are worth from $1 to $2 each; 1795, 1846 and 1838, without stars, if in good condition, are worth from 50c. to $1 each.

SMALL THREE CENT SILVER COINS.

All the issues of the Three Cent Silver Coins from 1863 to 1873 inclusive, in fine condition, from 15c. to 25c. each.

TWO CENTS COPPER COINS.

A fine specimen of 1873 coinage is worth 50 cents.

COPPER CENTS.

The rarest are the Copper Cents issued in 1793, 1799 and 1804, provided they are in a good condition, they bring from $3 to $5 a piece; but if in fine they sell at higher prices. The Copper Cent of 1809, if in a good state of preservation, is worth 50c. each. The cents with the following dates: 1794, 1795, 1796, 1797, 1800, 1805, 1806, 1808, 1811, 1813, and 1823, provided they are in good condition, bring a slight premium, but when in a poor or even only fair condition they are only worth their face value. Nickel Cent, 1856, $1.

HALF CENTS.

The issue of 1796 is worth $5 each; those of 1793 is worth $1, each; while those of 1794, 1795, 1797, 1802 and 1811 are worth from 25 to 50c. each, provided they are in a good state of preservation. 1831, 1836, 1840, to 1848 inclusive, 1849 with very small date, 1852, $3.50 each.

Of the United States Silver coins none of the other dates are rare, except those above mentioned and priced.

A. M. Smith, Numismatist, Philadelphia, Pa.

Colonial and Continental Paper Money.

As early as 1791, during the progress of King William's War, it appears that Massachusetts issued bills of Credit to pay her troops, Connecticut, New York, and New Jersey followed in train, in 1709, and issued the money to pay the

THE UNITED STATES
No 0,767 Forty Dollars.
This Bill entitles the Bearer to receive Forty Spanish milled Dollars, or the Value thereof in Gold or Silver according to a Resolution passed by Congress at York town 12th March 1778
CONFEDERATION
XL DOLLARS.
Continental Currency
FORTY DOLLARS

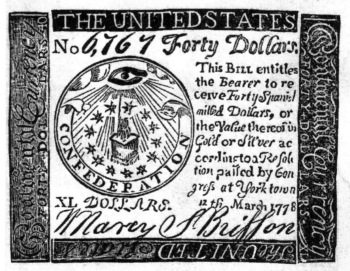

expenses of Indian Wars. The Legislature of Georgia issued paper bills of Credit that amounted in 1760, to seven thousand four hundred and ten pounds sterling. Each of the other Colonies resorted to the same means to raise money. Vermont issued the least amount, all of which appeared in one month

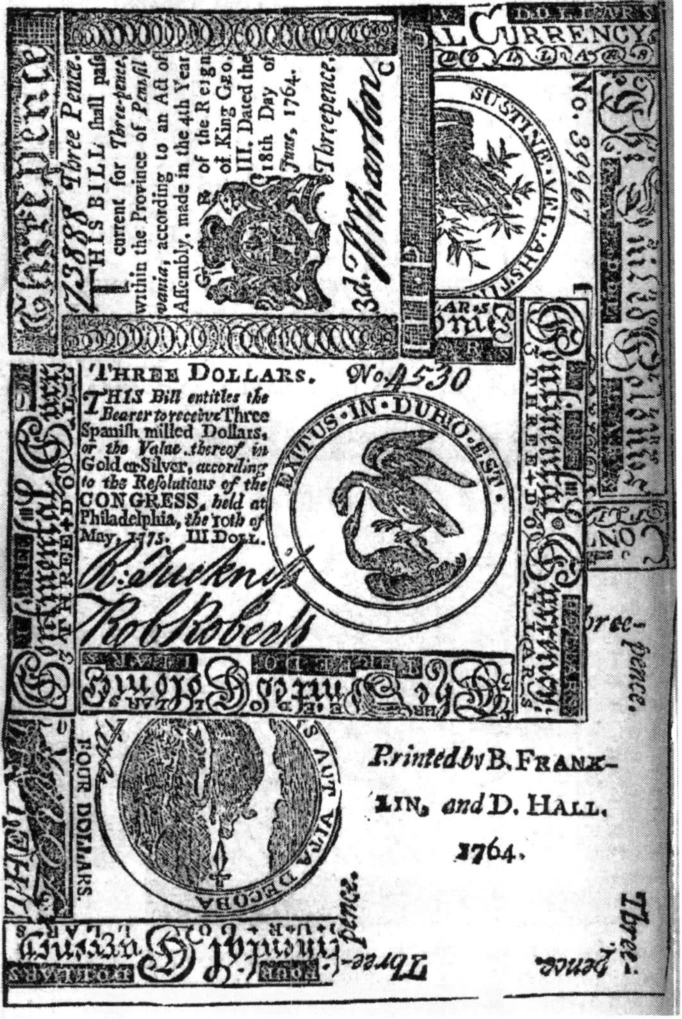
THREE DOLLARS.
No. 4530
THIS Bill entitles the Bearer to receive Three Spanish milled Dollars, or the Value thereof in Gold or Silver, according to the Resolutions of the CONGRESS, held at Philadelphia, the 10th of May, 1775. III DOLL.
EXITUS IN DUBIO EST.
Printed by B. FRANKLIN, and D. HALL. 1764.

1781, and was all redeemed. Other States redeemed it in
rt. The following list shows the time each of the Colonies,
in one instance the State, ceased to emit this paper money :

ew Hampshire,	1780	Pennsylvania,	1785
assachusetts,	1785	Delaware,	1777
aode Island,	1786	Maryland,	1781
mnecticut,	1791	Virginia,	1781
ew York,	1786	North Carolina,	1785
ew Jersey,	1786	South Carolina,	1779
	Georgia,	1786	

The first emission of bills of credit by congress was in June,
'75. The amount was two millions of dollars. Eighteen months
terward, twenty millions of dollars more were issued; and
ill later, a larger quantity; in all, three hundred and seventy-
ve millions. The states also issued many millions. In 1780,
: least two hundred million of continental money were in
irculation,

The confederation was indeed pledged to redeem these bills,
ad each colony its proportion of them, by the year 1779.
Nevertheless, they began to lose their value in 1777, and by
he year 1778, five or six dollars of it would only pass
or one.

But this was only the beginning of its depreciation. In
779, twenty-seven or twenty-eight dollars of it were only
vorth one of hard money, and in 1780 it was fifty or sixty
or one. By the middle of this year, the bills almost ceased
o circulate; and when they did circulate, it was at less than
i hundredth part of their nominal value, sometimes less than
he five hundredth.

Yet congress had ordered that they should be a lawful
ender for the payment of debts, at their full nominal value,
and the soldiers were to be paid in them. Six months' pay
of a soldier, in 1779, would not provide bread for his family
for a month; nor the pay of a colonel "purchase oats for
his horse."

There were many causes which operated to produce this un-
heard-of depreciation of a currency which the nation was
bound to redeem. 1. Too much of it was issued. 2. The
quantity was greatly increased by counterfeits and forgeries.
3. It was for the pecuniary advantage of public agents—since
they received a commission proportioned to the amount of
their purchases for the army—to pay high prices. 4. There
was a doubt of the ability of the states to pay these notes,
as well as a distrust of the faith of the states, in respect to their
redemption.

But whatever the causes may have been, and however promising its first effects, no measure of congress produced, more mischief in the end, by weakening and destroying public confidence, than this same continental money. It may be difficult, however, to say by what other means the war could have been sustained.

PLACES OF INTEREST TO VISITORS.

Academy of Fine Arts, Broad and Cherry Streets, admission, 25 cents. Lovers of Art should not fail to visit it.

Academy of Natural Science, Nineteenth and Race Streets. It contains 300,000 specimens. Admission, 10 cents. No one should fail to see it.

Carpenter's Hall, south side of Chestnut, below Fourth.

Custom House, south side of Chestnut, above Fourth.

Fairmount Park and Water Works. Go and see it by all means, or you will regret it.

Franklin's Grave, S. E. corner of Fifth and Arch Streets, can be seen from the street.

Girard College, Twentieth and Girard Avenue. Admission free, by tickets from the Ledger Offiice.

Independence Hall and National Museum, Chestnut Street, from fifth to sixth Street.

Laurel Hill Cemetery, the Oldest and Finest, in the United States.

Markets are spread all over the city, a visit to them will sufficiently repay you for your trouble, Wednesday or Saturday morning.

U. S. Navy Yard, south end of Broad Street.

New City Hall, Broad and Market, north of U. S. Mint. It is the finest in the United States.

Pennsylvania Hospital, Eighth and Spruce. Visitors admitted from 9 A. M. to 6 P. M. except on Saturday and Sunday.

Pennsylvania Museum and School of Industrial Art, is in the Memorial Hall, West Fairmount Park. Open from 9 A. M. to 6 P. M, except Monday. Admission free.

U. S. Naval Asylum, Gray's Ferry Road and Bainbridge Street.

Zoological Garden, on the west side of the Schuylkill River near Girard Avenue Bridge. Several thousands of wild beasts, birds and reptiles may be seen here. Admission, 25 cents.

CIRCULAR.

ESTIMATING AND PROCLAIMING, IN UNITED STATES
MONEY OF ACCOUNT, THE VALUES OF THE STAN-
DARD COINS IN CIRCULATION OF THE VARIOUS
NATIONS OF *THE WORLD.*

1881.
Department No. 1.
Secretary's Office.

Treasury Department,

BUREAU OF THE MINT.
Washington, D. C., Jan. 1, 1881.

Hon. JOHN SHERMAN,
    Secretary of the Treasury.

SIR:—In pursuance of the provisions of Section 3564 of the
Revised Statutes of the United States, I have estimated the values of
the standard coins in circulation of the various nations of the world,
and submit the same in the accompanying table.

                Very respectfully,

                    HORATIO C. BURCHARD,
                          Director of the Mint.

                TREASURY DEPARTMENT,
                  Washington, D. C., Jan. 1, 1881.

    The following estimation, made by the Director of the Mint, of the
value of the foreign coins above mentioned, I hereby proclaim to be
the values of such coins expressed in the money of account of the
United States, and to be taken in estimating the values of all foreign
merchandise, made out in any of said currencies, imported on or
after Jan. 1, 1881.

                    JOHN SHERMAN,
                       Secretary of the Treasury.

Estimate of Values of Foreign Coins.

Country	Monetary Unit.	Standard.	Value in U.S. Money	Standard Coin.
Austria	Florin	Silver	.4,07	
Belgium	Franc	Gold and Silver	.19,3	5, 10, and 20 francs.
Bolivia	Boliviano	Silver	.82,8	Boliviano.
Brazil	Milreis of 1000 reis	Gold	.54,6	
British Possessions in N. America	Dollar	Gold	$1.00	
Chili	Peso	Gold and Silver	.91,2	Condor, doubloon and escudo.
Cuba	Peso	Gold and Silver	.93,2	1-16, 1-8, 1-4, 1-2 and 1 doubloon.
Denmark	Crown	Gold	.26,8	10 and 20 crowns.
Ecuador	Peso	Silver	.82,3	Peso.
Egypt	Piaster	Gold	.04,9	5, 10, 25, 50 and 100 piasters.
France	Franc	Gold and Silver	.19,3	5, 10 and 20 francs.
Great Britain	Pound Sterling	Gold	4.86,6½	½ sovereign and sovereign.
Greece	Drachma	Gold and Silver	.19,3	5, 10, 20, 50 and 100 drachmas.
German Empire	Mark	Gold	.23,8	5, 10 and 20 marks.
India	Rupee of 16 annas	Silver	.39	
Italy	Lira	Gold and Silver	.19,3	5, 10, 20, 50 and 100 lire.
Japan	Yen	Silver	.88,8	1, 2, 5, 10, and 20 yen, gold and silver yen.
Liberia	Dollar	Gold	1.00	
Mexico	Dollar	Silver	.89,4	Peso or dollar, 5, 10, 25, and 50 centavo.
Netherlands	Florin	Gold and Silver	.40,2	
Norway	Crown	Gold	.26,8	10 and 20 crowns.
Peru	Sol	Silver	.82,3	Sol.
Portugal	Milreis of 1000 reis	Gold	1.08	2, 5 and 10 milreis.
Russia	Rouble of 100 copecks	Silver	.65,8	1-4, 1-2 and 1 rouble.
Sandwich Islands	Dollar	Gold	1.00	

CPSIA information can be obtained
at www.ICGtesting.com
Printed in the USA
BVHW051752050622
638960BV00003B/37